Tear-Free in Disneyland

TEAR-FREE
IN DISNEYLAND

A PARENT'S GUIDE TO LESS STRESS AND MORE FUN FOR THE WHOLE FAMILY

Second Edition

David W. Edgerton

Tear-Free in Disneyland
A Parent's Guide to Less Stress and More Fun For the Whole Family
Copyright © 2011 David W. Edgerton

First Edition, September 2011
Second Edition, May 2013
Published in the United States by David W. Edgerton
tearfree.disneyland@yahoo.com

ISBN: 978-1484843703

Every effort has been made to ensure the accuracy of information throughout this book and the contents herein are believed to be accurate at the time of publication. However, the author and publisher cannot accept responsibility for errors, omissions, changes or for consequences of any reliance on the information provided in this guide.

This book makes reference to various Disney characters, trademarks and products which are owned by The Walt Disney Company and/or Disney Enterprises. The author and publisher are not associated with the Disneyland Resort, The Walt Disney Company or any of the other companies, agencies or products mentioned in this book.

The following are trademarks, registered marks, and service marks owned by Disney Enterprises, Inc.: Adventureland®, Alice in Wonderland® Astro Orbiter®, Audio Animatronics®, Big Thunder Mountain Railroad®, Critter Country®, Disney California Adventure™ Park, Disney Junior® Live On Stage!, Disney's FASTPASS®, Disney's Grand Californian Hotel® & Spa, Disney's Paradise Pier® Hotel, Disney's PhotoPass®, Disneyland® Hotel, Disneyland® Park, Disneyland® Resort in California, Dumbo® the Flying Elephant, Enchanted Tiki Room, ESPN® Zone, Fantasmic, Fantasyland®, Frontierland®,, Good Neighbor® Hotel, Indiana Jones™ Adventure, "it's a small world," Main Street, U.S.A.®, Mickey's Toontown®, New Orleans Square®, Pirates of the Caribbean®, Sleeping Beauty® Castle Walkthrough, Soarin' Over California™, Space Mountain®, Splash Mountain®, Star Tours®: The Adventure Continues, The Haunted Mansion®, The Little Mermaid®: Ariel's Undersea Adventure, Tomorrowland®.

A Bug's Life, Cars, Finding Nemo, Monsters, Inc., Brave, Toy Story and Up characters: © Disney Enterprises, Inc./Pixar Animation Studios. Tarzan™ and Tarzan's Treehouse™ Owned by Edgar Rice Burroughs, Inc. The Twilight Zone® is a registered trademark of CBS, Inc. Winnie the Pooh: © Disney. Based on the "Winnie the Pooh" works by A.A. Milne and E.H. Shepard. Jack Skellington inspired by Tim Burton's Nightmare Before Christmas. The Muppets: © The Mupppets Studio, LLC. Facebook® is a registered trademark of Facebook Inc. Roger Rabbit characters© Walt Disney Pictures/Amblin Entertainment, Inc. Iron Man is a trademark of Marvel Entertainment, LLC.

For Deanna and Alex
Thank you for showering my life with pixie dust!

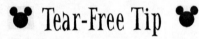 Tear-Free Tip

Join Tear-Free in Disneyland online for attraction closures, Disneyland rumors, upcoming events and shows, more tear-free tips, and to share your Disneyland stories and magical memories.

facebook.com/TearFreeInDisneyland

twitter.com/TearFreeDisney

Contents

Forward xi

Introduction xv

Why a "Tear-Free" Guide? 17

Glossary 19

How Young is Too Young? 21

Tear-Prevention Plan 23

Planning a Great Stay 29

The Parent's Ride Guide 37

The Best Time to Visit (And How Much it Costs) 77

Where to Stay 85

Disneyland Dining 91

Preparing Your Child 101

Money-Saving Tips 107

Special Services 115

Fun Finds 125

Useful Sites & Numbers 133

Ride Height Quick-View Guide 137

Forward

As a therapist and parent educator, I have worked with thousands of families in a variety of settings – happy families, sad families, foster families, adoptive families and families who defy an easy description. And, almost without exception, every family I've worked with has dreamed of going to Disneyland and having the time of their lives. They'd save their dimes, buy their airline tickets and then begin to build impossibly high expectations of the perfect Disney experience.

I cannot tell you how many horror stories I have heard from families about trying to have the "perfect" day at Disneyland. I remember one mother confessing to me, "Our family had more fun in the hotel pool than we did at Disneyland." Many of these stories have common themes – the kids get too tired, too scared, too bored standing in line, too hungry, too overwhelmed, and then the tears and tantrums erupt. In each case, the parents were surprised by, and totally unprepared for, the challenges of taking their family to Disneyland. Sadly, most of these problems could have been avoided with just a little research and planning.

In my opinion, The Walt Disney Company should make *Tear-Free in Disneyland* required reading before parents are allowed to buy tickets to the "happiest place on earth." This concise guide (short enough that even the busiest parent can read it) will make you laugh, save you time and give you the biggest bang for your buck.

Tear-Free in Disneyland is packed with tips and facts that help parents find the activities at Disneyland that best match their child's unique interests and stage of development. After all, a 6-year-old child will want and need a different day at Disneyland than a 12-year-old child.

So, take the few hours and read this book. Then create your own custom-tailored Disneyland itinerary. It's sure to pay off big when your kids (and you!) have a relaxing, fun and tear-free time.

And that means fewer horror stories for me – so everyone wins!

Linda L. McDaniels, MSW
Parent Trust for Washington Children

"To all who come to this happy place: welcome! Disneyland is your land. Here age relives fond memories of the past... and here youth may savor the challenge and promise of the future. Disneyland is dedicated to the ideals, the dreams, and the hard facts that have created America... with the hope that it will be a source of joy and inspiration to all the world."

– Walt Disney

Introduction

I'll never forget my first trip to Disneyland. I was in my mid 20s and had dreamed of going for, oh, about 20 years.

The moment I arrived I could feel Disneyland casting its spell on me. Gentle strains of familiar Disney tunes floated down from carefully hidden speakers, the scent of cotton candy and popcorn mingled in the breeze to create an irresistible perfume, while the smiles of excited children made the sunny California morning even brighter. I was hooked; and I hadn't even stepped through the main gate.

Once inside, I knew I'd lost my heart to Disneyland forever. My feet longed to run through the park as fast as they could, but my heart held their pace so that I could drink in every detail. From the charming nostalgia of Main Street, U.S.A. to the twinkling spires of Sleeping Beauty Castle, I was awed by the charm, the storytelling – the magic – that makes Disneyland exceptional among theme parks.

Now, 20 years (and more than a dozen Disneyland trips) later, I am no less enamored with the experience. I've had the great fortune to guide friends, family and especially my children through "the happiest place on earth." As I shared my love and knowledge of the resort with more people, I found myself turning into an unofficial Disneyland travel consultant. Arms loaded with park maps, schedules and notes, I'd joyfully help my friends plan their trips. The problem was, I had too many tips and ideas for one or even two consultations. I started writing longer and longer notes and emails, until it became clear that what I was really writing was a book.

The result is this compilation, which started as a way to make sure kids have a good time at Disneyland but is really just as much for parents. After all, every kid deserves a tear-free day at Disneyland – even the grown -up ones.

Why a "Tear-Free" Guide?

As parents, we want to share the promise of Disneyland's magic with our children. We're eager to see their faces light up with delight and wonder. So, we pack up the young ones and dash to the park expecting a "Zip-a-Dee-Doo-Dah" day. Instead, some of us are stuck dragging around a bunch of crying, red-faced, inconsolable monsters. So much for "the happiest place on earth."

Even on my very first trip to Disneyland, I seemed to spot them everywhere: the tear-stained faces of children. Tears at Disneyland? It seemed impossible. Who could be unhappy here? What's wrong with those kids? What's wrong with their parents? After years of observation and study (and having become a parent myself), I realized that it's not the kids' fault. And it's not the parents' fault either. It's simply a lack of experience and planning. But really, just how much planning is needed beyond hotel reservations and park tickets? Well, when young children are involved, plenty.

Look at it this way: you'd never dream of taking kids on a three-day hike up a mountain without plenty of preparation. Instead, you'd anticipate changing weather conditions, map out your route, plan meals and talk about safety. You'd explain to the kids what to expect on the hike, including the good (wildflowers and s'mores), the bad (tired legs and bugs) and the ugly (scary sounds and pooping outdoors). Well, a trip to Disneyland isn't as rugged, but it isn't any less challenging.

Does that mean you shouldn't take young children to Disneyland? Of course not! With just a little knowledge, a little planning and a few handy tips, you can head to Disneyland confident that your children (and you) will be able to experience the joys, thrills, fun and magic of Disneyland... without tears.

Glossary

Like most people, I most often refer to the entire Disneyland Resort (Disneyland Park, Disney California Adventure Park and Downtown Disney District) as simply "Disneyland." When discussing individual sections of the resort, I'll refer to them by their proper name (e.g., Disneyland Park). Here are a few other frequently used terms you'll want to know before proceeding:

- Audio Animatronics = Robotic animal or human figures
- Annual Passport = Year-round entry ticket
- Attraction = Usually a ride or theatrical event
- Blackout Dates = Dates closed to some passport holders
- Cast Member = Any Disneyland Resort employee
- Character = Any costumed Disney character
- Guest = Any visitor to the Disneyland Resort (you!)
- FASTPASS = Reduces long lines by reserving a return time for specific attractions (Free service)
- PhotoPass = Stores photos taken by Disneyland Resort photographers for later purchase
- Rider Switch Pass = Allows adult riders to take turns on a height-restricted ride while one waits with a child

How Young Is Too Young?

The first question most parents ask me is, "What's the best age to take my child on their first trip to Disneyland?" The answer, of course, is different for each child.

I've seen children at Disneyland so young, I was sure they were born while in line for Space Mountain. The babies I've seen at Disneyland don't really enjoy, appreciate or remember the experience. And their mothers don't exactly look like they're having a blast either. You'll usually find these exhausted moms near the exit to an attraction waiting, stone-faced, for their spouse (and possibly other children) to come out. Good times.

That said, there are many reasons why you may be visiting while you still have a babe in arms. If you do, there's one accessory I strongly recommend – grandparents. Yes, Grandma and Grandpa always seem ready to help with the baby (in fact, just try to stop them). They'll give mom and dad the freedom, time and energy to relax and have fun with the older children and each other.

If grandparents aren't handy, try to plan your trip with another family with children. Each set of parents can take turns entertaining the littlest ones while the other set takes the older kids on rides.

Of course, age isn't the only consideration. A child's temperament is also an important factor to think about.

- Is your child afraid of the dark? Many attractions take riders through dark, spooky passages. If so, you can stick to outdoor rides.
- Can he or she differentiate real from make-believe? Simulated flames, explosions and other pretend dangers will be found on many attractions.
- Does your child enjoy costumed characters? If meeting birthday clowns or Santa Claus was a traumatic experience, don't force a meeting with Captain Hook or Mickey Mouse.
- Can he or she be patient? From the line to get into the park, to rides, parades and fireworks, there's enough waiting to try the patience of any child (and most adults for that matter).
- Is your child comfortable with large, boisterous crowds? Expect a seemingly constant and heightened level of energy, noise and activity.
- Does he or she understand the word "no"? Children will be tempted by a parade of toys, costumes, keepsakes and goodies. Explain beforehand what your child's treat allowance will be and stick to it.

Answering no to any of the above questions doesn't necessarily mean your child isn't ready for Disneyland. But understanding how your child will react to these situations will help you anticipate their emotional needs and prepare them for the new experiences they'll encounter at the park.

Tear-Prevention Plan

It seems that every time I've witnessed a child crying at Disneyland, it was due to one of four common reasons, which I've dubbed "the FADE" (Fear, Anger, Disappointment and Exhaustion).

The truth is, unless you can borrow your fairy godmother's magic wand, we know it will be impossible to evade the FADE all the time, but you can minimize its occurrence by being prepared.

Understanding and anticipating how your child will react to the excitement, stimulation and stress of a Disneyland visit is the first step. Consider his or her feelings and reactions when planning your trip, and you'll find it's easy to avoid a lot of unpleasantness. And for those times when tears are unavoidable, you'll be better able to solve the situation calmly and understandingly – effectively diffusing the situation before it worsens.

"F" is for Fear

Disneyland Resort is rightfully famous for its kid-friendly atmosphere and family-oriented fun. But like any new experience, it also has plenty that might frighten younger children. Think about some of those Disney

animated classics. Most of the time it's sweet songs and
butterflies. Then, BANG! Bambi's mother gets shot. It's
part of the story, but it often comes as a surprise to parents and kids alike. To help understand how your child
will perceive the magical world that Disneyland presents, try looking at it through his or her wide eyes.

Like those animated movies, the most "innocent"
ride may surprise little ones with dark passages, explosive effects or wicked queens. Will these things frighten
your child? Consider his or her reaction to the villains in
a movie like "Snow White" or "Star Wars." Now imagine seeing the evil witch "come to life" on the dark ride,
Snow White's Scary Adventures or seeing Darth Vader
face-to-face at the Tomorrowland Jedi Training Academy. If your child enjoys the little thrills and frights
that come in movies like these, you probably don't have
anything to worry about. If you think it's best to avoid
them, there's still plenty to enjoy.

If you're not sure how your child will react to a ride,
you can try to lessen the shock by telling him or her what
to expect. For instance, in the Haunted Mansion, all the
guests enter a room (really an elevator) while a narrator
introduces the ride. When the elevator stops, the lights
go out momentarily and a lot of guests scream. This is
when I've seen quite a few surprised kids cry. But then
the lights come back on, the doors open, and people proceed to the loading area. So why not prepare your children beforehand by letting them know that everyone is
supposed to scream and that you'll let them know when
it's time? This allows them to anticipate and participate
in the spooky fun of the attraction.

Besides rides (attractions, in Disney parlance), there
are many other things that could frighten little ones.

- Characters, including pirates and Disney villains
- Live animals such as horses
- Screams (mostly from enthusiastic guests on rides)
- Fireworks, explosions and flame effects

"A" is for Anger

It's natural to think that our kids will spend their entire time at Disneyland brimming with joy, enthusiasm and, of course, gratitude for being taken there in the first place. But emotions get the best of us all. Don't be surprised if children get whiny or angry. It could be for any number of reasons.

They may be jealous because an older sibling gets to go on an attraction that they're too small to ride. They could be upset that they don't get a toy or sweet that they desire. They could just lose it because they've been pulled around all day and they have to do what everyone else wants to do. Now I'm not suggesting that you give in or pander to your children's demands simply to avoid a meltdown. Instead, remain calm and try to follow these simple do's and don'ts.

Don't

- Trivialize: "You're just tired."
- Bargain: "If you behave, you can pick the next ride."
- Bribe: "You'll feel better after an ice cream."
- Bully: "If you don't snap out of it, we're leaving!"

Do

- Listen: "Tell me why you're angry."
- Sympathize: "I see why that would upset you."
- Explain: "These are the rules."
- Share: "I'll sit here with you until you're ready."

Of course, if this approach doesn't work, there's always a good old-fashioned time out. If that's the case, try to find a nice shady spot where you can both sit and relax until everyone is calm. Once the moment has passed, forget about it and get back to the fun.

"D" is for Disappointment

On a recent trip, while my daughters and I waited in line to see the princesses at the Princess Fantasy Faire, we saw a nearby girl burst into tears when a Cast Member informed her that Pocahontas was not one of the princesses scheduled to appear. Her mother tried to comfort her, but the child was inconsolable. I truly felt for them both.

Meeting Pocahontas was clearly important to the girl, and providing that experience was important to the parent. Both left the area looking dejected. I can't help but think that both mother and daughter would have had a totally different experience if only they knew what to do before their visit.

• If there's a character your child is aching to meet, call Guest Relations (714) 781-4565 or stop by at City Hall on Main Street, U.S.A. Ask when and where (or if) your child's favorite character will be appearing. Certain characters (Mickey Mouse, especially) have specially designated meeting places. You can also meet many popular characters at Character Breakfasts or similar events. If the desired character is not on an appearance schedule, make sure your child understands that there's a good chance they won't see them. At the very least, you can ask a Cast Member if your child's favorite character will be appearing in any parades or shows during your visit.

• Check the Disneyland online calendar to see which attractions (rides) will be closed for updates or maintenance during your stay.

• Don't build unrealistic expectations or make promises you can't control. Attractions sometimes close unexpectedly. Fireworks shows get canceled due to high winds. It rains. Lots of things can happen that will require the whole family to be flexible and understanding.

"E" is for Exhaustion

It's easy to get caught up in the excitement of Disneyland. There's so much to see and do. But make no mistake; a day at Disneyland is an exhausting expedition.

You'll be walking hither and thither across 85 acres (and that's not counting Disney California Adventure Park). If you're there during summer, expect plenty of that famous Southern California heat and sunshine. And if you're anything like me, hot + tired = crabby.

Feet will hurt, legs will ache and tempers will get short. That is, unless you do what it took me many trips to learn: schedule breaks and rest periods throughout the day – and stick to them! Trust me, this is as much for you as it is for the kids.

• Take a 15-minute break every two hours. Find a shady spot to sit, relax and hydrate. And no, standing in line for a ride does NOT count as a break. Grab a cool drink and a snack, and find a comfortable spot. These breaks are a great time to appreciate the beautiful park grounds, people watch, or look at the park map and decide what to do next.

- Plan a 2- to 3-hour break in the middle of the day. Go back to the hotel, have some lunch, lie down or take a dip in the pool. You'll be amazed how pleasant the afternoon and evening can be when your body's batteries have been recharged.
- Bring or rent a stroller. Besides giving little legs a rest, strollers are a must for carrying around a bag with extra clothes, sunscreen, snacks, water, etc.
- Stick to your home routine. Meals, snacks, naps and bedtime should be the same at Disneyland as they are at home (more on this in the next chapter).
- Communicate. Tell everyone the day's schedule.
- Don't stay out too late. It's better to leave wanting more than staying to the bitter end and carrying exhausted, crabby kids (plus souvenirs) back to the hotel.
- Remember travel time. It will take at least as much time to get back to the hotel as it took you to get to the park in the morning – but it will feel much longer at the end of the day.

❤ Tear-Free Tip ❤

Get an app. There are several Disneyland mobile phone apps available with maps, show times, accurate wait times for attractions and dining reservation tools. For the official app, be sure to search for Disney's Mobile Magic.

Planning a Great Stay

When I first visited Disneyland over 20 years ago, I just showed up and figured out what to do once I got there. Of course, I was (relatively) young, childless and ready for anything. But time and kids change everything. Now I wouldn't dream of making the trip without carefully planning each day's schedule, complete with meal plans and rest breaks.

Now, don't worry. You don't have to schedule every second of every day. But if you do, be sure to leave time for spontaneity.

When planning your trip, there are a few things you'll want to consider in advance. How many days will you be in the area? How many of those days do you want to visit the Disneyland Resort? Which other Southern California attractions do you want to visit? Will your hotel be on Disneyland Resort property? Will you need a car? Your budget and preferences will probably determine a lot of these decisions, but I do have several recommendations.

• Get a hotel as close to the parks as possible. If you can afford it, stay at one of the Disneyland Resort hotels. You'll save a lot of time getting to and from the parks, which will make your entire stay more pleasant. My family typically stays at one of the Good Neighbor hotels right across from the main entrance. They're more affordable, and we love being able to just walk across the street to our room for breaks and at the end of a long day.

- Don't drive to the parks unless you have to. Shuttles go between most of the nearby hotels and the resort. But note that the shuttles can get crowded during peak times and sometimes fill up. You can also expect your shuttle to stop at several hotels going to and from the park, so plan your time accordingly. If you do decide to drive, understand that the Disneyland Resort parking garage is still a distance (a free tram ride away) from the park.

- Decide where and when you'll eat. Eating inside the parks is fun and convenient, but it can also get pretty expensive. We usually have at least one meal per day inside the parks. The rest of the time we eat at one of the family-style restaurants near the resort. Many hotels serve a complimentary continental breakfast, which is a real time and money saver in the morning.

- When you do dine in the parks, either make reservations or plan to eat early. Lunch and dinner times in the parks can get crazy busy. And the rush tends to run late. To avoid the crowds, have lunch at 11:00 a.m. and dinner at 4:00 or 5:00 p.m.

- Wondering which attraction has the shortest line? Download one of the many mobile phone apps that show you accurate wait times or check the reader boards on Main Street, U.S.A. and Buena Vista Street.

- Schedule a little "wild time" every day. There are a couple of great places in both parks where kids are encouraged to safely run free and go crazy (and parents can join in or sit back and watch the fun). Disneyland

Park has Pirate's Lair on Tom Sawyer's Island with trails, caves to explore and fun places to climb. Disney California Adventure has Redwood Creek Challenge Trail with rope bridges, lookout towers and even a rope swing.

• Make time for grown-up fun. If there are two or more adults present, give each other a little break away from the kids so you can each shop, go on a grown-up ride or just sit quietly. A great time to do this is during "wild time."

• Come early. Leave early. The morning hours at the park are some of the most enjoyable. The crowds tend to grow throughout the day, so morning is the best time to enjoy those "can't miss" rides. I prefer afternoons and evenings for watching parades and catching shows. I do not, however, recommend getting to the park before the official opening time unless you have a Magic Morning early admission ticket. Crowds gather early and you'll have to stand around waiting for the park to open. Instead, arrive just as the gates open. The lines will already be moving and you'll be in the park before you know it.

• If your hotel or travel package includes a Magic Morning early admission ticket – use it! You and a small group get to enjoy certain sections of the park for a full hour before the general crowds come rushing in.

• Bring what you need but don't carry more than you have to. If you don't need your entire purse, leave it at the hotel. I always leave my wallet in the hotel safe. I just tuck some cash, park tickets, I.D., cell phone, one credit card and my hotel key in a pocket. If there are items you do need but don't want to lug around, you can rent a locker on Main Street, U.S.A.

Here's a sample of the type of schedule I typically work up for one of our family trips. If we're there for more than a few days, I'll include other amusement parks such as Universal Studios, Legoland or Sea World. For some trips, we'll reserve a whole day to lounge at the

SAMPLE PARK PLAN

Check resort schedule for operating hours, ride closures and parade/show times. Call (714) 781-3463 for reservations at full-service restaurants inside the resort

	DAY ONE	DAY TWO	DAY THREE
7am	In-room Breakfast		
8am	Disneyland Park opens	Character Breakfast Goofy's Kitchen	Disneyland Park opens
9am	Fantasyland	California Adventure Opens	Adventureland and Frontierland
10am		Cars Land	
11am	↓	↓	↓
Noon	Lunch Village Haus Restaurant	Lunch at Ariel's Grotto (12:15 Reservation)	Lunch Hungry Bear Cafe
1pm	Toon Town	A Bug's Land Rides	New Orleans Square
2pm			
3pm	↓	↓	
4pm	Hotel (naps & swim)	Hotel (naps & swim)	Hotel (naps & swim)
5pm		↓	
6pm	Dinner Outside Park (Mimi's Cafe)	Dinner Boardwalk Pizza & Pasta	Dinner Rainforest Cafe
7pm	6:30 Parade	Paradise Pier Rides	Critter Country New Orleans Square
8pm	Tomorrowland	↓	
9pm	↓	World of Color Show 9:15	Fantasmic 9:00
10pm	9:30 Fireworks Return to Hotel	Return to Hotel	Return to Hotel
11pm			
MidN			

hotel or go boogie boarding at one of Southern California's incredible beaches. If you have time and you want to experience quintessential SoCal, be sure to include an excursion to Hollywood, the Santa Monica Pier and Venice Beach. You'll never run out of fun things to see and do.

OUR VACATION PLAN

	DAY ONE	DAY TWO	DAY THREE
7am			
8am			
9am			
10am			
11am			
Noon			
1pm			
2pm			
3pm			
4pm			
5pm			
6pm			
7pm			
8pm			
9pm			
10pm			
11pm			
MidN			

If you're flying into the area, be sure to include your flight times in your schedule as well as travel time to and from the airport. This will help you accurately predict how much time you can spend at the parks and when you need to depart.

OUR VACATION PLAN

	DAY FOUR	DAY FIVE	DAY SIX
7am			
8am			
9am			
10am			
11am			
Noon			
1pm			
2pm			
3pm			
4pm			
5pm			
6pm			
7pm			
8pm			
9pm			
10pm			
11pm			
MidN			

- Skip the camera. These days, I don't bother with a separate camera. I just use the one built into my phone. That way I can send a picture to Grandma or upload it to Facebook right from the park. For special keepsake photos, I use the photographers stationed at landmarks around the parks. They take much better photos than I do and the whole family gets to be in them. The first time they take your photo, they'll give you a PhotoPass card. Just hand it to any official photographer, and all your photos will be immediately available for purchase (prints or CD) on Main Street, U.S.A. and online.

- Bring a few small toys and games. A doll, action figure or book can be a great way to occupy fidgety kids while they're waiting in line for a ride or for a parade to start. However, do not bring that favorite, irreplaceable toy in case it gets lost or left behind.

- Pack a snack. Officially, outside food and drinks are not allowed except in cases of food allergies (hint-hint). However, we usually bring in a few granola bars and water bottles and have never had any problems. They do check all bags before you enter the park, so don't bring more than you need.

- Dress for the season. Sunscreen, hats and sunglasses are summertime musts. Light jackets are usually sufficient for cool morning hours. When we return to the park in the evening, we either bring sweatshirts or buy them at the park as part of our souvenirs.

- Stick as close to your home routine as possible. Time away from home is full of new experiences and can be very stressful for everyone involved, especially kids. Nap time, bath time, meal time and story time are all ways you can assure them that there's still order and predictability in their world.

• Relax and have fun! Okay, this last one seems obvious, but it can be easy to let the crowds and the desire to get your "money's worth" out of each day push you and your family beyond your limits. There are lots of special moments that happen throughout the day (character sightings, parades, musical performances, etc.). So avoid the temptation to get so rushed that you end up missing the little things that make a day at Disneyland so magical. Your goal shouldn't be an attempt to fit more "stuff" into the day – but rather to get more enjoyment out of the day.

❤ Tear-Free Tip ❤

Don't miss your favorite thrill rides just because you've got a little one along. When you get to the front of the line ask the Cast Member for a Rider Switch Pass. This allows parents to ride one at a time while the other waits with the child. Be sure to explain to your child ahead of time that this ride is for Mommy and Daddy only and give them something to do while they wait.

A Parent's Ride Guide

On a friend's recent trip to Disneyland, the very first ride she took her 3-year-old son on was Mr. Toad's Wild Ride. It's a fun, silly car ride through a cartoon landscape. Seems innocent enough, right? Sure, except that all the "crashing" through walls and explosive sound effects frightened the boy enough that he didn't want to go on any more rides. Not a total disaster, but an unlucky choice for the first ride of the visit. Of course, in time he came around, but his understandable reaction demonstrates the importance of knowing what to watch out for.

The first thing you should consider is your child's height. Many rides have minimum height requirements and Disney Cast Members are sticklers for this rule. If your child doesn't reach the minimum height, he or she will not be allowed on the ride. And I've never seen any amount of crying or cajoling change a Cast Member's mind. Prior to going on your trip, measure your child and check the Tear-Free Ride Rating Guide in the next section to see which rides have a minimum height requirement. Even if there are some rides your child is too small to ride, don't worry; there's plenty to see and do.

Once you know which rides your kids are able to go on, it's time to consider which ones they are ready (and want) to go on. Are they afraid of the dark? Do they get anxious around fire or startled by loud noises? Consider your child's temperament and disposition before suggesting a ride. Most parents have a pretty good idea what will trigger fear and anxiety in their child. But in some cases you'll just want to ask.

When my youngest girl was 6, she was game for any ride they'd let her on – even ones that loop-de-loop. For

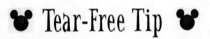

🐭 Tear-Free Tip 🐭

If you're flying in, Santa Ana Airport (a.k.a. John Wayne/Orange County Airport) is much closer to Disneyland Resort (a $35-$45 cab ride) than LAX. Be sure to ask your hotel if they have a free (or can recommend a discount) airport shuttle.

her, the scares were part of the fun. I encourage you to let your children test their own limits (so long as it's safe of course). You might be surprised by how brave they can be. Still, it's not a bad idea to let them know what to expect from the ride and from you. For instance, you can say, "Now, this ride might get dark at times. But I'll be with you the whole time. Okay?" To help you know what you and your child can expect, I've prepared a list of attractions with brief descriptions.

Tear-Free Ride Rating Guide

☺ A-Okay! Tear-Free fun for virtually everyone.

😐 Maybe. Questionable or a few scary elements.

☹ No Way! Intentionally thrilling and / or scary.

Disneyland Park

Making its debut in 1955, Disneyland was conceived as a place for parents and their children to enjoy together. But it's so much more than a collection of rides – Disneyland is a truly immersive experience that makes guests feel as if they've stepped out of the regular world and into a place of imagination and magic. It's this magic that makes Disneyland a place families have cherished for generations.

Last time I counted, there were over 50 attractions within Disneyland Park. To be clear, an attraction can be a ride (like the Jungle Cruise), a play area (like Goofy's Playhouse) or a theatrical presentation (like the Enchanted Tiki Room). And, the vast majority of attractions are suitable for young children. Still, it's best to know which attractions you'll want to avoid and which ones you'll most want to go on or see (and in what order) so you can have a Tear-Free day.

Main Street, U.S.A.

This welcoming thoroughfare is a charming replica of a "typical" American town in the early 1900s. Here, you'll find guest services, shops and plenty of places to buy sweet treats.

In the morning (particularly during peak seasons) don't be surprised to see one or more Disney characters ready to welcome guests, sign autographs and pose for pictures.

Many of the shops on Main Street, U.S.A. are open for an additional hour after the park has officially closed. They tend to get pretty crowded as people head out of the park, so try not to your leave souvenir shopping to the last minute.

The Disney Gallery
(All ages)
Part art gallery, part gift shop, visitors can view illustrations, prints, sculptures and paintings that served as inspiration for Disneyland resort attractions and/or the art of Disney movies. New, temporary exhibits appear frequently, so there's often a lot to see that's new. Visitors can purchase prints, books and reproductions of many of the sculptures that appear there.

Disneyland Railroad
(Dark tunnel, dinosaurs, simulated thunder)
This biofuel-powered steam engine train ride, with stops in New Orleans Square, Mickey's Toontown and Tomorrowland is a fun and relaxing way to get around the park. Stay aboard for the tunnel between Tomorrowland and Main Street Station – you'll see life-size dioramas of the Grand Canyon and even dinosaurs.

Main Street Cinema
(Darkness)
Pretend to take a ticket from Tilly in the ticket booth and step inside this old-fashioned movie house to introduce the kids to some vintage Mickey Mouse cartoons. The theater has 6 screens in a circle playing continuous loops of black and white Mickey Mouse shorts from his early

career. Just be advised that there are no seats in this theater, it's always "standing room only."

Main Street Vehicles
(Live horses, ringing bells, horns)
Take an old-fashioned one-way trip from Main Street's Town Square to Sleeping Beauty Castle (or back) on a horse-drawn streetcar or carriage, a double-decker Omnibus or a vintage fire engine.

Great Moments with Mr. Lincoln
(All ages)
This theatrical presentation starts with a brief slideshow about America's early struggles and ends with a stirring speech from an animatronic Abraham Lincoln. Walt Disney Imagineering (then called WED Enterprises) created Mr. Lincoln for the 1964 New York World's Fair. In the pre-show lobby, you'll find a mini-museum with art and artifacts from Disneyland's early days and Walt's office much as he left it.

 Tear-Free Tip

Main Street, U.S.A. is home to the Disneyland First Aid Station and Baby Care Center. You'll also find a handy ATM and locker rentals. Guest services (including guided tours and dining reservations) are right inside City Hall.

Adventureland

Take the first left off Main Street and you'll find yourself in another time and place with exotic jungle-themed adventures around every corner. This is one of Disneyland's original lands – with the Jungle Cruise remaining virtually unchanged since its 1955 premier.

😊 Enchanted Tiki Room
(Birds, simulated thunder and lightning)
Your family is sure to enjoy this charming animatronic musical revue performed by birds and flowers. The show ends with a crash of thunder, lightning and a simulated rainstorm outside. While waiting for the show to start, we always pick up a Dole Whip pineapple frozen dessert to share.

😞 Indiana Jones Adventure
(High speed, darkness, fire, simulated bugs and danger)
This ride is not for the meek. You'll ride a screeching, careening Jeep across rickety bridges, pass by giant snakes and barely escape a rolling boulder. No wonder it's a favorite among older kids and thrill-seeking adults. If the line is long, use the decoder below to read messages carved into the walls. (Minimum height 46" / 117cm.)

Jungle Cruise
(Water, wild animals, simulated gunfire)
Your friendly skipper will take you on a pun-filled and gentle cruise through exotic jungle rivers. Have your camera ready for the animatronic tigers, elephants and apes that appear on the shores. And keep your eyes on the waters–they're teaming with animatronic crocodiles, hippos and piranhas. The cruise seems slightly more sinister in the dark of night, but it's still a lot of fun.

Tarzan's Treehouse
(Heights, stairs, animal noises)
Climb the stairs up into Tarzan's jungle home. As you explore, it's easy to see the remains of the ship that brought Tarzan's family to Africa's shores. Near the top, you'll find a growling statue of a jungle cat, but most find this a fun walk through the treetops. Some parents may remember this as Disneyland's Swiss Family Robinson Treehouse. As you exit, be prepared to wait as your kids join in a musical jam session banging on pots, pans and other "percussion instruments."

 Tear-Free Tip

By mid-day, Adventureland gets so packed with people that it's difficult to even wend your way through it (especially for strollers and wheelchairs). If the Jungle Cruise is on your list of things to do, then visiting this area before noon is your best bet.

Frontierland

Take a trip to the Old West. This is one of Disneyland's smaller "lands," but it's packed with plenty of character. Rustic buildings, desert landscapes, an old-fashioned shooting gallery and live entertainment bring the Old West to life.

Head to the Golden Horseshoe Saloon for live entertainment from bands like Billy Hill and the Hillbillies every day of the week.

☹ Big Thunder Mountain Railroad
(High speeds, steep drops, tight turns, darkness)
Hold on to your hats and glasses – this high-speed roller coaster not only has spine-tingling dips and hair-raising turns, it also goes through a dark, rumbling cave with tumbling boulders that some kids will find frightening. (Minimum height 40"/102cm.)

☺ Big Thunder Ranch
(Live animals)
Follow the paved trail along the far side of Big Thunder Mountain Railroad and you'll come across Big Thunder Ranch. In this shady and naturalistic setting, you'll meet and have the chance to pet a cute collection of barnyard animals including goats, sheep and pigs. This is also the site of many holiday-themed festivals, carnivals and live entertainment events.

☻ Fantasmic!
(Disney villains, flame effects, loud noises, cannon fire)
This live, nighttime performance is viewed from the banks of the Rivers of America in New Orleans Square. It's full of fun and fantasy but also contains more than its

share of scary elements and special effects. If you plan to see this show and don't have reserved seating, ask a cast member to help you pick out a good viewing spot and stake your claim at least an hour before show time. It won't start until after dark, and many small children are fast asleep before the show begins, so this show may be just for the grown-ups.

Frontierland Shootin' Exposition
(Simulated gunfire)

This is an old-fashioned shooting gallery using infrared beams of light instead of buckshot to hit the targets. Targets, such as tombstones and buildings in a miniature frontier town, light up or become animated when hit. This is one of Disneyland's few attractions that cost extra money to play.

Mark Twain Riverboat/Sailing Ship Columbia
(All ages)

A great way to escape the heat and crowds, these calm and enjoyable ships take travelers on a trip around the Rivers of America. The recorded voices of river guides point out special landmarks and discuss the historical significance of the ships. Some special animatronic scenes on the banks of the rivers can only be seen from these boats.

Pirate's Lair on Tom Sawyer Island
(All ages)

Take a short raft ride across the river and prepare to let the kids run and play. There are trails, pontoon bridges, climbing areas and spooky caves for adventurous kids of all ages.

❣ Tear-Free Tip ❣

As you depart Frontierland, walk towards the Rivers of America. You'll soon spot the remains of a huge petrified tree. This ancient artifact is believed to be between 55 and 70 million years old!

New Orleans Square

The first stop of the Disneyland Railroad, New Orleans Square is a beautiful and festive area bristling with the spirit of the "Big Easy." I don't know if it's the architectural detail, the shady spots to rest or the lively jazz music, but New Orleans Square is one of my favorite places to just sit and people watch. Stroll down shop-lined alleys and stop for a bite of gumbo (or a sweet beignet). Some of the attractions might not be suitable for small children, but if your kids wants to meet a pirate, there's a good chance they'll meet one here.

😐 Haunted Mansion
(Darkness, screams, spooky images)
Knowing how your child reacts to the spookier aspects of Halloween should give you a good idea if they're ready for the Haunted Mansion. Though it's dark throughout, the singing ghosts in this haunted house keep things from getting too scary. That's not to say it's completely scare-free. There are plenty of ghosts, cobwebs, coffins and spooky sounds (even my own mother wouldn't ride on it). One of the scariest bits may be the elevator

ride down. At the end of the introduction, the lights go out and guests tend to scream. Prepare your child and have them scream along so they're part of the spooky fun instead of a victim of it. From October through New Years, Jack Skellington takes over and transforms this attraction into a jolly Nightmare Before Christmas.

🙂 Pirates of the Caribbean
(Darkness, steep drops, simulated fire/gunfire)
While the pirates do partake in a bit of skullduggery (including sword and gunplay), this attraction is mostly harmless fun. But be prepared, the boat will go over a few short, dark waterfalls. Some children may find the realistic-looking flame effects distressing. Keep an eye open for Captain Jack Sparrow – he makes several appearances throughout the attraction.

❤ Tear-Free Tip ❤

New Orleans Square is also the seating area for the popular evening show, "Fantasmic." This makes it almost impossible to get through the area prior to or during scheduled performances. If you're not going to see the show, avoid New Orleans Square and Critter Country after dark.

Critter Country
Just past New Orleans Square is Critter Country. There aren't many attractions in this charming woodland area, but here you're almost sure to meet Winnie the Pooh, Eeyore, Tigger and their friends.

Davy Crockett's Explorer Canoes
(All ages)
A fun way to see the Rivers of America is by paddling along with other guests and two expert "explorers." Initially, I thought this attraction looked dull and had to be coerced into going. But once aboard, I was immediately enamored with it. Even on hot days, it feels cool on the water and the views of the riverbanks are lovely. As long as no one in your party is afraid of boats or water, it shouldn't be a problem. Operates seasonally.

 The Many Adventures of Winnie the Pooh
(Simulated thunder and lightning)
A sweetly gentle ride through Winnie the Pooh's animated adventures. Other than some mildly menacing Heffalump imagery, and a few thunder and lightning effects during Pooh's blustery day, this ride is a charmer. Older riders may remember this location was once home to Country Bear Jamboree, and Max, Buff and Melvin from that attraction can still be found inside.

 Splash Mountain
(Steep drops, darkness, high speed, splashing)
Not only will you experience this attraction's famously frightening five-story plunge, but also other smaller waterfalls and dark passages. But, if you and some of the bigger kids are brave enough, you'll be rewarded with a real thrill. Oh yeah... there's also a pretty good chance that you'll get splashed. If one or more of you parents want to ride Splash Mountain, you can use the single rider line (usually a much shorter line) or ask the attraction's Cast Member for a Rider Switch Pass (one parent at a time rides while the second parent waits with the child). (Minimum height 40" / 102 cm.)

❤ Tear-Free Tip ❤

Critter Country is a dead-end. To get anywhere else, you'll have to retrace your steps through New Orleans Square. If your next destination is Toontown, Tomorrowland or Main Street, take the Disneyland Railroad from New Orleans Square.

Mickey's Toontown

Mickey's Toontown is a favorite of younger visitors, but this crazy cartoon town is fun for all ages. There's a good chance you'll see Goofy, Minnie Mouse and some of their friends. Be sure to visit Mickey Mouse's house, where you can meet the "big cheese" in person.

☺ Chip 'n Dale Treehouse
(All ages)
Kids can climb up the twisting staircase to get a chipmunk's-eye view of Toontown.

☺ Donald's Boat
(All ages)
Another brief walk-through attraction, the S.S. Daisy is a great place for kids to peek through Donald's periscope, pretend to steer the ship and generally blow off a little steam.

Gadget's Go Coaster
(Steep drops and fast turns)

Though this ride looks like a "kiddie" coaster, it moves very quickly with tight turns. It's a fairly short ride, so if the wait time is long, come back later. (Minimum height 35"/89cm.)

Goofy's Playhouse
(All ages)

Explore Goofy's wacky garden and colorful house. Here, jumping on the furniture isn't just allowed – it's encouraged. Cushy foam coverings make this a fun and safe place for kids to get a little goofy.

Mickey's House and Meet Mickey
(All ages)

Get an up-close look inside the home of the world's most famous mouse. As you exit, you have the option to visit Mickey's "Movie Barn" where your child can meet and have his or her photo taken with the "big cheese" himself. Though the line to meet Mickey can get long, it moves fairly quickly and you get to watch cartoon clips while you wait. The Disney photographer on-hand will take pictures with their camera or yours, so you can get in on the fun too!

Minnie's House
(All ages)

Like Mickey's house, Minnie's is full of cute photo opportunities and interactive displays. Stop by for a cup of "tea," and see what Minnie has cooking in the kitchen. You can let kids know that Minnie said it's okay to poke around, press buttons and turn knobs on the gadgets they see. You never know what'll happen in Toon Town.

Roger Rabbits' Car Toon Spin

(Darkness, recorded screams, strobe lights)

Turn the wheel (like in the teacup ride) to make your car spin "out of control" as Bennie the Cab takes you on a wacky tour of Roger Rabbit's world. Lot's of good fun, but the creepy weasels and other sinister characters make the wait line and ride fairly spooky.

 # Tear-Free Tip

There's not much in the way of dining options in Mickey's Toontown, but it's a fun place for a light lunch or snack. Grab a hot dog, ice cream bar or cool drink, and rest your feet while you people watch. Be sure to stop by my favorite hat shop in Disneyland.

Fantasyland

Fantasyland provides the greatest number of options for younger guests in one area. Its fairytale theme, frequent princess sightings and large variety of Disney-themed carnival rides make this area a must-see for kids and parents alike.

 Alice in Wonderland

(All ages)

Except for some fairly dark passages, this is a sweet and gentle ride. Kids familiar with the Disney animated film will enjoy passing by singing flowers, the Red Queen's silly croquet game and the Mad Hatter's tea party.

Casey Jr. Circus Train
(All ages)
You don't have to be a train-lover to enjoy a ride on this circus train. The slightly elevated tracks treat parents and kids to the magically miniature villages of Story Book Land on one side and a view of Fantasyland on the other. Look carefully and you might see that some of the train cars are actually refurbished carrousel seats from the original King Arthur Carrousel.

 Dumbo the Flying Elephant
(Spinning, heights)
Kids of all ages enjoy taking to the sky in their own flying elephant. A simple-to-operate joystick allows you or the kids to make Dumbo fly higher and lower.

 Fantasy Faire
(All ages)
Just left of the drawbridge to Sleeping Beauty Castle is a magical little village populated by a rotating roster of Disney's most popular princesses. Stop by The Royal Hall to meet three princesses in person. Signs tell you which princesses are available and the expected wait time. Little (and big) visitors will have a chance to chat and take photos with each one. Nearby, The Royal Theatre presents live reenactments of popular Disney princess stories while Maurice's Treats offers sweet and savory twisted bread snacks and frosty apple blend beverages.

 Fantasyland Theater
(All ages)
This outdoor amphitheater is just steps away from the Toontown station of the Disneyland Railroad. Here, you

can take a load off your feet and enjoy live recreations of Disney animated classics and new, original shows. No tickets or reservations are required to see the performances and seating is first-come-first-served, so the earlier you arrive, the closer to the stage your seats will be. Check your daily schedule to see what's playing and for show times.

 "it's a small world"
(All ages)
Don't listen to the world-weary cynics who claim the repeating song on this ride will drive you crazy. This classic Disneyland attraction is bristling with charm and whimsy. Thanks to the recent refurbishment of this attraction, you'll now find the famous singing "dolls of the world" joined by 30 famous Disney characters (including Aladdin, Alice, Belle, Pinocchio, Simba, Woody and Jessie) in their country of origin. Can you spot them all?

 King Arthur Carrousel
(All ages)
Unlike most carrousels, every horse on the King Arthur Carrousel is a "jumper." That is, every horse moves up and down in a galloping motion as the carrousel turns. Built in 1875, the carrousel also features a large bench for those who don't wish to ride a horse.

 Mad Tea Party
(Spinning, dizziness)
This attraction is quintessential Disneyland. Turn the wheel to make your teacup spin faster (or slower, if you wish). Even without turning the wheel, this ride is a dizzying trip that kids of all ages enjoy. A stationary teacup

sits just outside the attraction's exit, ready for photographs.

🙁 Matterhorn Bobsleds
(High speed, steep drops, sharp turns, darkness, eerie noises)
Older kids love this wild bobsled ride through icy caverns and past rushing waterfalls. The easily frightened should also be warned that the abominable snowman lurks inside the mountain. (Minimum height 42" / 107cm.)

🙂 Merida and Friends
(All ages)
Near "it's a small world" you'll come across a little piece of Scotland from the Disney/Pixar film, Brave. Luckily, you've arrived just in time for a festival! Spin the wheel to learn which clan you belong to, do crayon rubbings and color characters from the film and see who has the best aim in bean-bag toss. You can even try your hand at the bow and arrow. (A safe and kid-friendly version, of course.) You'll even have the chance to meet Merida with her little brothers still in the form of mischievous bear cubs.

🙂 Mr. Toad's Wild Ride
(Darkness, strobe lights, sharp turns, explosion and flame effects)
Mr. Toad's car goes careening through Toad Hall, into town and even into the fiery underworld. Younger guests may find the frenetic energy of this attraction a bit much, though most find it all in good fun.

☺ Peter Pan's Flight
(Darkness, simulated flight)

A gently flying pirate ship takes riders out the nursery window and high over the twinkling lights of London. Once your ship arrives in Neverland, you'll see an animatronic Peter fence with Captain Hook before rescuing Wendy and the other children.

☺ Pixie Hollow – Tinkerbell & Her Fairy Friends
(All ages)

While you wait in line for this character meet-and-greet, you'll notice something strange. Are the plants getting larger? No, you're shrinking down to fairy size! But don't worry, right after you've had a chance to meet Tink, Periwinkle, Vidia and their friends, you'll grow back to normal size. Look for Pixie Hollow on the outskirts of Fantasyland, near the Tomorrowland side of Sleeping Beauty Castle.

☺ Sleeping Beauty Castle Walkthrough
(Darkness, confined area, simulated flame, spooky images)

Ever wish you could go inside Sleeping Beauty Castle? You can! Just past the castle's entrance on the left is a rather unassuming door beneath an awning. Once inside, you'll take a walking tour past enchanting dioramas showing scenes from the classic Disney film. Some of the scenes and a shadow of Maleficent at the end can feel menacing. There are quite a few stairs in the walkthrough, but an alternate (video) experience is also available.

Rapunzel and Flynn Ryder
(All ages)
Look for the tall tower with long blond strands cascading out the window – it can only be the home of Rapunzel. Inside her fancifully painted room, you'll find the golden-tressed adventurer and her friend, Flynn Rider. Stop by for a brief chat, photo opportunity and an autograph. With very little prodding, Flynn will show you "the smolder."

Snow White's Scary Adventures
(Darkness, haunted woods, menacing witch)
The ride starts sweetly enough inside the home of the Seven Dwarfs as Snow White heads to bed. From there, you're meant to experience the ride as Snow White. You'll pass through a sparkling jewel mine before heading into the dark and spooky woods. You'll see several images of the evil queen in her disguise as the old hag as she tries to temp you with an apple. These scenes are brief and, of course, the witch gets it in the end.

Storybook Land Canal Boats
(All ages)
Gentle canal boats take passengers on a narrated tour of the most famous little lands inside Disneyland. See Pinocchio's village, Cinderella's castle, Toad Hall and more, recreated in miniature. The surrounding grounds are beautifully landscaped with live miniature trees and shrubs. This is one of my favorite attractions (I just love miniature things!). But like many attractions in Fantasyland, the line gets insufferably long on busy afternoons. The little buildings and grounds are also beautifully lit in the evening, but I prefer to see it during the daytime for the best view.

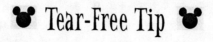

Tear-Free Tip

Due to its popularity, Fantasyland tends to become a stroller freeway from mid-day to late in the evening (traffic jams and fender benders are inevitable) so early hours are best. While waiting in line for Peter Pan's flight, watch the window above the entrance to the Snow White attraction to see the evil queen.

Tomorrowland

Race into the future in one of Disneyland's most vibrant and exciting areas. Popular with teens and adults for its thrill rides, Tomorrowland also has plenty to offer younger guests.

 Astro Orbiter
(Heights)
Using a simple joystick, little astronauts can control the height of their own rocket ship as it spins around the galaxy. Give your young one the controls and let him or her be in charge of this simple and enjoyable ride.

Autopia
(All ages)
With mom or dad operating the accelerator, even small kids can safely steer these gas-powered cars through a winding freeway. This popular attraction usually draws long lines, but once you get going, it's a ton of fun. (Minimum height 32"/81cm and 54"/137cm to drive alone.)

Buzz Lightyear Astro Blasters
(Darkness, strobe lights, large robots)
Ride through a maze of aliens and robots and rack up points as you fire your "laser pistol" at targets. Some creatures, including a larger-than-life Evil Emperor Zurg, may frighten some, but for the most part, it's a fast-paced and fun shooting gallery that kids love.

 Captain EO Starring Michael Jackson
(Scary sci-fi villains, danger and action)
This 1986 3-D musical adventure features Michael Jackson at the height of his career on a spectacular movie adventure (directed by Francis Ford Coppola with George Lucas serving as executive producer). Captain EO and his rag-tag crew of aliens face off against the wicked Supreme Leader (Angelica Huston in disturbing alien/spider regalia). Naturally, Michael uses the unstoppable power of music and dance to save the day.

 Disneyland Monorail
(All ages)
Take a ride around the Disneyland resort all the way to the Downtown Disney District. It's a fast, convenient way to get to the many shops and restaurants of Downtown Disney and the Disneyland Resort hotels. If you leave the monorail and plan to return to the park later, be sure to get a hand stamp.

 Disneyland Railroad
(All ages)
Board the steam-powered locomotive for a quick trip back to Main Street Station (with a quick detour through the Grand Canyon), or stay on board for stops in New Orleans Square and Mickey's Toontown.

Finding Nemo Submarine Voyage
(Confined quarters, appearance of being underwater)
See Nemo, Marlin, Dory and their friends on an undersea adventure. Don't worry about where you sit – both sides of the submarine are treated to identical views. Includes periods of darkness and some short unsettling scenes, but these pass quickly.

 Innoventions
(All ages)
This building is a showcase of new and emerging technologies including (not surprisingly) the latest Disney video games. Take a tour of the totally wired "home of the future" and even say hello to ASIMO, the remarkable human-like robot built by Honda. Temporary exhibits may show props, set pieces and costumes from high-tech Disney or Marvel films like Iron Man.

 Space Mountain
(Speed, darkness, strobe lights, steep drops, sharp turns)
This high-speed roller coaster is set inside a dark mountain with spinning stars and galaxies projected onto the night sky. Includes some strobe lights and one dizzying light effect near the end. (Minimum height 40"/102cm.)

 Starcade (Video Game Arcade)
(All ages)
A classic token-operated video arcade featuring over 200 old school and new arcade-style video games. It's a great place to introduce your kids to classic games like Pac Man, Frogger, Donkey Kong, Galaga and Centipede (assuming you're old enough to remember those yourself). Some, like Q*bert, they may recognize from Disney's "Wreck-It Ralph."

Star Tours: The Adventure Continues
(Simulated high speed, bumps, sci-fi action)
The recent conversion of this thrilling ride now means that riders can enjoy over 50 variations of pre-set adventures in 3D. (The movie has several changeable scenes, which are randomly selected so you can ride again and again and not have the exact same experience twice.) There's lots of space action and near-collisions with asteroids and other ships, but if the kids are big (and brave) enough, it's a lot of fun. Like many motion simulators, I find that the further back you sit, the rougher the ride. If you want a gentler ride, ask to be seated closer to the front. Be sure to keep your eye on the side monitors, there may be a rebel spy on board! (Minimum height 40" / 102cm.)

 Tear-Free Tip

When in Tomorrowland, be sure to check the schedule for events at the Tomorrowland Terrace Stage. During the day, young visitors can view or even participate in the Jedi Training academy and during summer nights visitors are treated to live music.

Disney California Adventure Park

When Disney California Adventure Park first opened in 2001, some visitors complained that it lacked the kind of magic that made the "real" Disneyland so remarkable. My family and I disagreed. We've been fans since our first visit. From the glamour of old Hollywood to the bustling wharfs of San Francisco and the peaceful redwood forests – we loved its quintessentially Californian – if quirky – charms (not to mention its less-crowded avenues). It did feel less "Disney" than its sister park, and some of the decor didn't suit my taste, but we all enjoyed its thrilling attractions, spirited parades and variety of dining options.

Now, thanks to a recent $1.1 billion expansion and renovation, Disney California Adventure Park is better than ever with all-new attractions, more restaurants, a "main street" modeled after 1920's Los Angeles – even an all-new Cars Land. The refurbished park comes to life with music, live entertainment and, of course, classic Disney characters. The result is real Disney magic.

Buena Vista Street

Once known as Sunshine Plaza, Buena Vista Street represents a time when Walt Disney first arrived in California to begin his fledgling animation studio. You'll stroll through an idealized version of old California, you'll find shops, refreshments (including a Starbucks) and Guest Relations, as well as stroller, wheelchair and locker rentals.

The new, iconic centerpiece of Buena Vista Street is the Carthay Circle Theater. It's famous in Disney lore as the theater where "Snow White and the Seven Dwarfs" made its world premier in 1937. This version of the Spanish Colonial Revival building (the original was demolished in 1969) houses a fine- dining restaurant, a cocktail lounge and 1901, a private club.

At the end of Buena Vista Street in Carthay Circle, look for "Storytellers," a life-size statue of a young animator named Walt Disney and his friend Mickey Mouse. It represents their arrival in California with little more than a suitcase and a dream to start a new animation studio.

Red Car Trolley
(All ages)
Step back in time to take a ride on the Red Car Trolley. Riders get a one-way trip through Hollywood Land. It's a fun way to travel between California Adventure's main entrance and the Twilight Zone Tower of Terror Hotel.

❤ Tear-Free Tip ❤

To see Disney's World of Color show, pick up free tickets for that evening's performance at the Grizzly River Run FASTPASS Service area or stop by Guest Relations to pre-purchase a meal with a reserved viewing-area ticket.

Hollywood Land

Pass through the "studio gates" and step back in time to visit Hollywood's golden age. Here, the buildings represent architectural icons of Hollywood Boulevard including the Beverly Wilshire Hotel and Chapman Market. They also hold an array of entertainment options for young visitors. And since you're in "Hollywood," don't be surprised if you spot Phineas and Ferb, Sophia the First and other "celebrities" ready to give autographs and take photos. At the far end of the street, the Hyperion Theater presents "Disney's Aladdin – A Musical Spectacular."

Disney Academy Building
(All ages)
Kids and grown-ups will have fun learning how animation works in four colorful, interactive settings. Kids can chat with their favorite Finding Nemo character at "Turtle Talk with Crush." Stop by the "Animation Academy" to take a drawing class with a real Disney animator. Down in the "Sorcerer's Workshop," kids can discover which Disney character their personality matches and lend their voice to a cartoon. While over in "Character Close-Up," they'll see how their favorite Disney characters go from simple sketch to living creation.

Disney Junior Live On Stage!
(All ages)
If your kids enjoy "Sofia the First," "Doc McStuffins," "Jake and the Neverland Pirates" or the "Mickey Mouse Clubhouse," they will love this fun, musical live show featuring Mickey and his Disney Junior friends. Floor seating encourages kids to jump up, sing and dance along with the show.

Disney's Aladdin – A Musical Spectacular
(All ages)
If you're a fan of the Disney's animated motion picture, "Aladdin," you're sure to enjoy this condensed live per-

formance. Full of dazzling sets, costumes and special effects, this is a show my family has enjoyed time and time again. The show-stopping number, "Friend Like Me," never fails to raise the roof. Entry is free with your park admission and reservations are not required. Seating is first-come-first serve, so show up well before show time if you want to sit closer to the stage. However, there are no bad seats in the Hyperion Theater.

🙂 Monsters, Inc. Mike and Sulley to the Rescue!
(Darkness, monsters, strobe light effects)
Follow nice monsters Mike and Sulley on a quick tour of Monstropolis as they hurry to rescue their human friend, Boo. If your child made it through the Pixar movie, "Monsters Inc.," he or she should have no problem with this ride.

🙂 Muppet*Vision 3D
(Darkness, frenetic energy, explosion effects)
This fun 3D movie also features animatronic Muppets and characters to create a "4D" experience. Some of the 3D effects realistically appear to come right at you, so young children may have a hard time remembering, "it's just a movie."

🙁 Twilight Zone Tower of Terror
(Darkness, steep drops, spooky atmosphere)
After wending your way through a haunted hotel lobby, a leery library and a forbidding boiler room, you'll ride an elevator that takes guests on a thrilling 13-story drop. It's not called the Tower of Terror for nothing! (Minimum height 40"/102cm.)

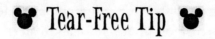

🐭 Tear-Free Tip 🐭

Once you pass the Hollywood Land entrance gate, look all the way down the street. It appears to go on forever, but it's just a bit of Hollywood magic at work. The painted backdrop at the end of the street is a perfect place for a family photo.

Cars Land

Just when you think Disneyland Resort couldn't get any bigger, they somehow find space to build a whole new land. Cars Land is a life-size recreation of Radiator Springs – the town made famous in the Disney/Pixar animated feature, "Cars."

This 12-acre area features amazing recreations of the buildings from the film as well as Cadillac Range and Ornament Valley. You'll feel like you stepped into the movie as you travel through striking desert landscapes, car-shaped mountains and graceful stone arches and partake in a variety of Cars-themed attractions, dining and shopping experiences.

This area is stunning during the daytime, but the drama really happens at night when the neon lights of Radiator Springs turn it into a magical masterpiece.

😊 Luigi's Flying Tires
(All ages)
This clever bumper car concept is a reinterpretation of

the Flying Saucer attraction that operated in Tomorrowland from 1961–1967. Riders climb inside a tire that floats on a cushion of air and lean to steer and gently bounce off other drivers. To operate this ride successfully takes coordinated teamwork. My family found we had more luck when there are two riders per vehicle (three makes it too hard to time the movements). On busy days, this attraction can be painfully slow to load but goes by very quickly when it's finally your turn. For that reason, I don't recommend getting in line unless the wait time is 20 minutes or less.

Mater's Junkyard Jamboree
(Tight turns, swinging motion)
Take a musical spin through Mater the Tow Truck's junkyard. Tractors tow guests riding in a trailer as they dance and swing you to-and-fro in tight circles. This is a simple, enjoyable ride like an old fashioned tilt-a-whirl (without the tilting). What makes it more fun are the silly square dance tunes sung by Mater during the ride.

Radiator Springs Racers
(High speeds, quick acceleration, sharp turns)
Get behind the wheel of your own racecar and get ready to speed through Radiator Springs. Fans of the Cars movies will enjoy the pre-race drive through Radiator Springs and getting a quick tune-up before racing through the stunning desert landscape. Your car will take hairpin turns and steep banks like a pro (no matter who's driving), but this ride is more thrilling than scary. You'll eventually race another car on the track, with the "winner" being randomly selected. (Minimum height 40" / 102cm.)

☙ **Tear-Free Tip** ☙

Tear-Free Tip: During busy periods, the lines for Radiator Springs Racers become insanely long. If large crowds are expected on the day of your visit, pick up a FASTPASS for Radiator Springs Racers first thing in the morning. During the summer, I've heard of this attraction's FASTPASS tickets running out by 10 a.m.

Grizzly Peak

Visit the rolling hills of California's wine country as well as its stony mountain tops, lush redwood forests and its aviation industry all within a few minutes walk. The state's natural and industrial heritages are celebrated in this area featuring woodland play areas, thrilling rides and delicious dining options. Standing guard above it all is the mountainous summit of Grizzly Peak, named for its resemblance to the ursine symbol of California.

☹ Grizzly River Run
(Wetness, sharp turns, steep drops)
There's a good chance you'll get a little wet (and quite possibly soaked) on this turbulent raft ride down a twisting river. Be prepared to go over splashing rapids and steep waterfalls. It's a real thrill and very refreshing on hot days. (Minimum height 42" / 107cm.)

Redwood Creek Challenge Trail
(All ages)
This enclosed woodland area is a great place to relax, explore and let the kids run wild. Climb a ranger's mountain observation tower, cross a swinging rope bridge and explore mountain caves. Russell and Dug (from Disney/Pixar's "Up") offer young adventurers challenges, mysteries and activities to keep little nature-lovers occupied and entertained. (Some height and age requirements for certain activities.)

 Tear-Free Tip

When your body's batteries are running low, visit the Redwood Creek Challenge Trail's Ahwahnee Camp Circle and ask a "ranger" when the next story time will be. Little kids will be entertained and you'll have a nice break.

Condor Flats

A salute to California's high-flying aviation industry, Condor Flats may be the smallest land in Disney California Adventure, but it contains one of its most beloved attractions. It also has a jet engine shaped mister to cool you down on scorching days.

 Soarin' Over California
(Heights, simulated flying)
Take a seated "hang glider" ride over famous California landscapes and landmarks. Ocean breezes and spe-

cial scents make the experience feel even more real. The beauty and fun of flying make this a must-see attraction. (Minimum height 40" / 102cm.)

Pacific Warf

Pacific Warf isn't so much a "land" as a collection of quick-service restaurants. This is a nice option when the family members can't agree on where to eat– everyone can pick their favorite (so long as you don't mind standing in more than one line). Options include Pacific Warf café with fresh soups and sandwiches– including soup in a bread bowl (my favorite). Enjoy grilled chicken, carne asada, tamales, burritos, tacos and enchiladas from Rancho Cucomonga Mexican Grill. Over at The Lucky Fortune Cookery you can choose from rice bowls featuring beef, chicken or tofu with sauces such as Mandarin orange , Thai curry, teriyaki and spicy Korean. If your sweet tooth is acting up, the Ghiradelli Soda Fountain and Chocolate Shop has the cure.

☺ The Bakery Tour
(All ages)
If you're at all curious how those tasty sourdough bread bowls get made, then head over to the Boudin Bakery Tour. A recorded video starring Rosie O'Donnel and Colin Mochrie tell you the history of sourdough bread while you watch bakers make the freshest bread in Disneyland.

☺ Walt Disney Imagineering Blue Sky Cellar
(All ages)
Across from the entrance to Cars Land and next to the Wine Country Trattoria restaurant, this frequently changing display offers visitors a sneak peek at the

exciting changes coming to Disneyland Resort. You'll see models, design sketches and videos explaining the Imagineering process and get a taste of things to come.

Paradise Pier

Resembling a Victorian-era seaside amusement park, this area contains lots of classic and enjoyable carnival rides plus a few that are thoroughly modern and a real thrill. You'll also find an assortment of popular midway games with Disney themes and prizes. Besides being the home of the nightly show "World of Color," the large water feature in Paradise Park is also home to Instant Concerts conducted by Goofy and accompanied by dancing fountains.

🙁 California Screamin'
(High speed, sharp turns, loop-de-loop)
Not for the very young – or the faint of heart – this thrilling coaster blasts off and goes from 0 to 55 mph in four seconds (uphill even)! There's also a thrilling 108-foot drop and a loop-de-loop. If the kids are tall enough and you decide to ride, be sure everyone keeps their head against the headrest so no one whacks their head during takeoff. (Minimum height 48" / 122cm.)

🙂 Duffy the Disney Bear
(All ages)
Near the entrance to Ariel's Grotto is a gazebo where fans of Disneyland's official teddy bear can meet the life-size version for autographs and photos. Stuffed versions of the cuddly bear and a wide variety of clothing options are available for purchase at shops around the resort.

Games of the Boardwalk
(All ages)
A variety of pay-per-play midway games give you and the kids the chance to test your skills and maybe win fun prizes. Magnet fishing, baseball toss, skee ball and water pistol-style games are the norm. Pre-paid cards make paying for games easy. Credits come in $5 increments (usually good for 2 plays).

 Golden Zephyr
(Heights, spinning)
Take a gliding ride as shining silver rocket ships spin you higher and higher. This gentle and enjoyable ride is a great way to catch a cool breeze on a hot summer day.

 Goofy's Sky School
(High speed, heights, sharp turns, steep drops)
Sharp twists, turns and sudden drops make this roller-coaster-style ride too intense for younger guests. Frankly, this ride scares the pants off me – but my kids just love it. (Minimum height 42" / 107cm.)

 Jumpin' Jellyfish
(Heights)
Jumping jellyfish take riders on a 4-story flight straight up before bringing them back–gently bobbing and floating–to earth. (Minimum height 40" (102cm)

 King Triton's Carousel
(All ages)
Ride seahorses, dolphins, flying fish, whales and other sea creatures on this beautifully designed merry-go-round.

The Little Mermaid: Ariel's Undersea Adventure
(Darkness, simulated underwater, villains)
Take a ride in your own personal clamshell buggy "under the sea." You'll see recreations of key scenes and hear snippets of all your favorite songs from the Disney animated classic, The Little Mermaid. Some smaller children may find the Ursula animatron with her undulating tentacles a little scary, but this ride is mostly a fun, musical romp.

 Mickey's Fun Wheel
(Heights, rocking, option for rolling gondolas)
Get a bird's eye view of the park from this 16-story tall Ferris Wheel. Unlike most wheels, this one has both stationary and rolling gondolas that glide on a track for a wilder experience. The swinging gondolas are a lot of fun but come with motion sickness bags for a reason. Most people (and kids) I know find the rolling gondolas too scary. The stationary gondolas do sway and rock, but offer a much gentler ride.

 Silly Symphony Swings
(Heights, spinning)
Another classic carnival ride – the kind where you take a spin in chairs suspended by chains. It's a lot of fun and you get a great view of the park below, but some kids (like me) may feel unnerved by the uncontrolled swinging motion. (Minimum height 40" / 102cm.)

 Toy Story Mania!
(Loud noises, quick action very stimulating)
Play 3D versions of popular midway games (toss darts at balloons, throw balls at plates and even throw pies) with your favorite Toy Story characters. This is one of

my family's favorites, but small riders may have trouble aiming the "cannon." Currently there's no FASTPASS available for this attraction and the line tends to get really long by afternoon. So try to go as early in the day as you can.

"a bug's land"

Based on the Disney / Pixar animated film, "A Bug's Life," this area was made especially for the little ones. Even the smallest kids can enjoy the pint-sized attractions and family-friendly entertainment. In fact, you'll feel insect-sized yourself as you walk among gigantic plants and oversized household items. Older kids (8 and up) might think the rides are a tad tame, but the area is so cleverly designed, there's sure to be something for everyone to enjoy.

😊 Flik's Flyers
(Heights)
Younger children will enjoy this gentle ride in a floating "hot air balloon."

😊 Francis' Ladybug Boogie
(Spinning)
A mini version of Disneyland's famous teacups ride, the faster you turn the wheel, the faster your ladybug spins.

😊 Heimlich's Chew Chew Train
(All ages)
This is a gentle train ride through an over-sized garden. It's fun to see the giant fruits and vegetables and you can even smell some of the treats.

It's Tough to Be a Bug!
(All ages)

When it's time for a break in "a bug's land," check out the "4D" movie, "It's Tough to Be a Bug." It's an entertaining combination of 3D movie plus animatronic characters and effects. Some younger viewers may be disturbed by darkness, strange smells, fog and spray effects as well as some of the more menacing insects that participate in the show.

Princess Dot Puddle Park
(All ages)

Kids can chase jumping water drops and frolic in the cooling sprays and dripping waters of oversized garden hoses. Kids are naturally attracted to this water-themed play area and it can be a great place to let them cool off if they're getting restless or too hot in the sun. If you're worried about them getting (and staying) wet, avoid this area in the cooler parts of the day or bring a small towel and change of dry clothes.

Tear-Free Tip

Looking for a shortcut between Cars Land area and the Twilight Zone Tower of Terror or the Hyperion Theater? Follow the road past Luigi's Flying Tires and cut through the far end of A Bug's Land. You'll end up at the far end of Hollywood Land where you can visit the attractions there or catch the Red Car Trolley back to Buena Vista Street.

☺ Tuck and Roll's Drive 'Em Buggies
(Bumping)

This is a slow-moving and fairly gentle version of the classic bumper car ride. Though appropriate for younger kids, many small children have difficulty steering these kinds of cars (they tend to over-steer), so an older rider or adult may want to ride along. (Minimum height 36"/91cm.)

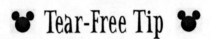

❤ Tear-Free Tip ❤

If mom or dad have some alone time and want to get in a few thrill rides, look for Single Rider signs or ask a cast member for a Single Rider Pass on the following attractions: California Screamin', Goofy's Sky School, Grizzly River Run, Indiana Jones Adventure, Radiator Springs Racers, Soarin' Over California, Splash Mountain. You'll proceed to the front of the line much faster.

The Best Time to Visit
(And How Much It Costs)

If you ask me (and if you're reading this chapter, you are), there is no bad time of year to visit Disneyland. However, some would disagree. Summers can be hot (and crowded), winter can be wet (and crowded) and spring can be... well you get the idea. Each time of year offers advantages and challenges.

On-Season

When kids are out of school, families flock to Disneyland – and for good reason. In summer, the days are sunny, the evenings warm and the park festivities are in full swing. But it's not just summer – weekends and holidays also draw large crowds to the parks.

To accommodate the multitudes, the parks stay open late into the evening. You'll also find longer wait times for rides, and traffic jams of people pretty much everywhere you go.

Still, if you love sunshine, you can't beat summer at Disneyland. (July and August are unbearably hot in my opinion, so go as early in the summer as you can.) Halloween is celebrated all October long with decorations and special events. And nobody celebrates the winter holidays like Disneyland. The decorations are spectacular, there are special parades and firework displays, and they even manage to make it "snow" on Main Street, U.S.A.

The on-season includes:
- Mid-June through Labor Day
- The weeks surrounding 3-day weekends
- Weeks before and after Easter (Spring Break)
- Thanksgiving Weekend
- Week before Christmas through New Year's Day

Off-Season

For parents of young children, I generally recommend visiting Disneyland "off-season." Late winter, early spring and early fall are the park's least busy times of year. This means fewer visitors, which translates into shorter lines. It can also mean less pleasant weather and shorter operating hours. But that can actually be a good thing. You'll be able to enjoy more of the parks and be back at the hotel in time for the kids' regular bedtime.

The day of week the can also make a big difference. The crowds tend to grow as the week progresses, so Monday through Wednesday are generally the best days to visit. The downside is that fewer visitors also mean fewer entertainment options. Some events, such

---

❤ Tear-Free Tip ❤

Holidays of many cultures are celebrated at Disneyland, including Dia de los Muertos and Chinese New Year. Check the Disneyland web site for scheduled events.

as parades, fireworks and shows like Fantasmic!, may only run on Fridays and Saturdays during the off-season. Just check the events calendar online and plan accordingly.

The off-season is also when Disneyland refurbishes some of its attractions. That could mean you'll find your favorite attraction closed for repairs, updating or painting. If you have a "can't miss " attraction like "it's a small world," The Haunted Mansion or Pirates of the Caribbean, check Disney's online calendar to see what's scheduled to be closed. Also, the weather can be a little iffy during these times of year. On those rare days when it does rain, keep rainproof ponchos handy (also available in the parks). Keep in mind, parades, fireworks and other events may be canceled during inclement weather.

The off-season includes:
- January through Mid-February (Presidents Day)
- Late April through the end of May (Memorial Day)
- Mid-September (after Labor Day) through Mid-October (Columbus Day)
- Thanksgiving through the week before Christmas

Between Season

This "non" season is officially considered off-season, but Disneyland is still a popular destination for California residents. Disneyland also holds numerous group events throughout the year. You'll find low-to-moderate crowds depending on the weather and whether or not there's a special event taking place.

The between-season includes:
- Late February through the week before Easter
- Sundays (except summer and holiday weekends)
- After Memorial Day until schools are out for summer
- Mid-October through Thanksgiving

How Many Days?

How long you plan to visit will have a lot to do with practical limitations.

• How many days of vacation do you have?
• What else do you want to see in Southern California?
• Do you have friends or relatives you want to visit?
• What will your budget allow?

But what parents really want to know is, "How many days at Disneyland do we *need*?" In my opinion, the answer to that is simple. At least three. You can (and I have) done Disneyland for fewer than three days, but that can feel rushed and be very tiring. But even when we've stayed in California for a full week, we rarely spend more than three of those days at the Disneyland Resort. The rest of that time is spent visiting other Southern California attractions like the San Diego Zoo, Legoland, Hollywood, Venice Beach and Universal Studios.

My preferred schedule usually includes two days at Disneyland Park and one day at Disney California Adventure. Of course, we may switch parks mid-day depending on when particular shows, parades and firework displays are happening.

On your first trip, it's important not to try to pack too many activities into too short a time. The key to an enjoyable vacation (anywhere) is to have plenty of time to explore, relax and have fun.

Also, don't be surprised if the kids just want to spend the afternoon splashing in the hotel pool or playing with a new best friend they just met. Be flexible and ready to shuffle your schedule to accommodate spontaneous fun.

Park Ticket Prices

The cost to enter the parks at Disneyland Resort varies throughout the year. Prices may also be discounted as part of a promotion or travel packages that include airfare and accommodations.

For your reference, I've included prices published on the Disneyland Resort website valid through 12/31/13. These prices may not be accurate by the time you wish to travel, but they should give you a good idea of some of the more popular options available and the prices you can expect to pay. Please note that each of the examples below is per-person.

1-Park Per Day Tickets

This style of ticket allows you entry into either Disneyland Park or Disney California Adventure (your choice). Whichever park you enter first is your park for the day. You may exit and return to the same park as many times as you want (be sure to get a hand stamp), but you cannot enter the other park on the same day without a separate admission ticket. This ticket is about $30 per person/per day less than a Park Hopper Ticket.

- 1-Day 1-Park
    - Ages 3 to 9: $81, Ages 10 & Up: $87
- 2-Day 1-Park Per Day
    - Ages 3 to 9: $158, Ages 10 & Up: $170
- 3-Day 1-Park Per Day (with Magic Morning)
    - Ages 3 to 9: $205, Ages 10 & Up: $250
- 4-Day 1-Park Per Day (with Magic Morning)
    - Ages 3 to 9: $225, Ages 10 & Up: $245
- 5-Day 1-Park Per Day (with Magic Morning)
    - Ages 3 to 9: $240, Ages 10 & Up: $245

Park Hopper Tickets

This more flexible ticket allows you to visit both parks each day of your ticket. You can go back and forth between Disneyland Park and Disney California Adventure as many times as you want in a single day (again, a hand stamp is required after your first entry). This is particularly handy if you want to spend most of the day in one park, but then dine or see an evening show in the other park.

- 1-Day Park Hopper Ticket
    Ages 3 to 9: $119, Ages 10 & Up: $125
- 2-Day Park Hopper Ticket
    Ages 3 to 9: $188, Ages 10 & Up: $200
- 3-Day Park Hopper (with Magic Morning)
    Ages 3 to 9: $205, Ages 10 & Up: $220
- 4-Day Park Hopper (with Magic Morning)
    Ages 3 to 9: $225, Ages 10 & Up: $275
- 5-Day Park Hopper (with Magic Morning)
    Ages 3 to 9: $270, Ages 10 & Up: $290

Annual Passports

These tickets allow you entrance to both Disneyland Park and Disney California Adventure Park throughout the year. Annual Passports are a single price for all guests ages three and older.

- Premium Annual Passport (No blackout dates)
    Ages 3 to 9: $649, Ages 10 & Up: $649
- Deluxe Annual Passport (315 pre-selected days of admission)
    Ages 3 to 9: $469, Ages 10 & Up: $469

Magic Mornings

When you purchase tickets for three or more days (or stay in a Disneyland Resort Hotel), you receive 1 Magic Morning early admission at Disneyland Park. This allows you to enter the park a full hour before the general public (only selected lands/attractions will be open). Despite the early wakeup call, I love Magic Morning early admission. It's a treat to see the park virtually free of people and it's a great way to get in several attractions before the park starts getting crowded. Check resort schedule for the hours and the availability of Magic Morning early entrance.

🖤 Tear-Free Tip 🖤

If you are a resident of Southern California, you may be eligible for special California offers. Check the Disneyland Resort website for details.

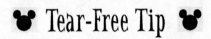

Tear-Free Tip

Here's a tip from Disneyland Cast Members: when you really want to communicate with your child, bend down to be at his or her height. You'll have their full attention without seeming forceful. Princesses, Characters and other Disneyland Cast Members do this regularly as a matter of policy to great effect.

Where to Stay

There's a lot to see and do in Southern California. You could spend days or even weeks visiting different beaches, Hollywood highlights, amusement parks and natural wonders – and let's not forget the reason we're all here – Disneyland. So, choosing where to stay during your visit can make a big difference in the levels of convenience, comfort and enjoyment you experience.

Friends & Family

If you and your family are invited to stay with friends or relatives in the Los Angeles area, you're sure to save a lot of money. But unless they live right there in Anaheim, you're also sure to spend a lot more time getting to and from Disneyland Resort than if you stayed in a nearby hotel. However, your hosts will probably have a lot of tips and insights for visiting the Southern California area, which is certain to come in handy. If you plan to drive yourself to the resort, give yourself extra time to fight morning traffic, park and travel from the parking area to the park (a 10-minute walk or short tram ride from the resort's parking garage). And I'm sure I don't need to remind you to be a good house guest. That way, you'll be sure to be asked back! And being a good house guest involves planning too. Here are a few tips to get you started.

- Prior to accepting the invitation, ask about sleeping arrangements to make sure you and your host family will all be comfortable.
- Provide your own transportation (if you didn't drive there, rent a car). This not only keeps you from troubling your hosts, but also allows you to do things on your own schedule.
- Learn their daily routine so that you're not keeping them up or making them late for work.
- Don't expect them to be your tour guide. However, do invite them to join some of your activities.
- Let your host know your daily schedule so they know when you'll be coming and going from the house.
- Do your own family's laundry, dishes and clean up after yourselves.
- If you feel it's not working out, preserve the peace by moving your family to a hotel.
- Show your appreciation with a gift the host family can enjoy or by taking them out for a special meal.
- Return the favor– invite them to stay with your family.
- Don't overstay your welcome. Remember the old adage, "fish and house guests go bad after three days."

Disney Resort Hotels

If it fits in your budget, I can think of no better place to stay than one of the hotels within Disneyland Resort. The Disney theme carries through hotel lobbies, restaurants and right into the guest rooms. And they're all walking distance or a short monorail ride away from

---

❤ Tear-Free Tip ❤

If a room with a view is an important part of your hotel experience, be sure to mention it when making your reservation. Pool and park-view rooms may cost a little more, but they're a lot more pleasant than the standard view of the parking lot.

---

the parks. In each Disneyland Resort hotel you'll find specially-themed swimming pools for the kids, spas and fine dining for the adults, children's story time and special activities in hotel lobbies and character meals in many of the restaurants.

The least expensive of the three is Disney's Paradise Pier Hotel. Its recent remodel evokes the feeling of seaside resort and boasts a rooftop swimming pool complete with water slides. Some of the rooms have views of Disney California Adventure Park. Choose 1 and 2 bedroom suites or single room options with one king bed or two queen size beds.

For a little more money you can stay at the Disneyland Hotel. It's also been recently remodeled with smart contemporary styling in its public areas and guest rooms. The highlight of each room is a fiber optic headboard that sends you to sleep with a private firework show. If you really want to splurge, check out the hotel's luxury suites. There's a Pirates of the Caribbean Suite, the Adventureland Suite, a Fairy Tale Suite, a Big Thunder Suite and even the Mickey Mouse Penthouse! There are 1 and 2 bedroom suites or single room options with one king bed or two queen size beds.

My favorite (and the most costly) is the Grand California Hotel & Spa, which has its own entrance right into the Disney California Adventure Park (no line!). The rooms are large and evoke the rustic craftsman style of a California mountain resort. Family-friendly room options include one, two or three bedroom suites or single rooms with a king size bed, one queen size bed plus a bunk bed or two queen size beds.

Your stay at a Disneyland Resort hotel may cost more than some of the surrounding options, but it could be worth it for the added convenience and extra fun. For a basic room with 2 queen size beds, you're looking at around $301/night for Paradise Pier Hotel, $409/night for Disneyland Hotel and $474/night for Grand California Hotel & Spa. (Rates based on 6-night stay, 2 adults, 2 children booked in early summer 2013.) As an added bonus, Disneyland Resort hotels frequently come with little extras such as FASTPASS tickets and Magic Morning early admission tickets. These hotels do fill up during peak seasons, so be sure to check availability months in advance of your trip. Check the Disney web site or call (714) 956-6425 for availability and rates.

Good Neighbor Hotels

Disneyland Resort is surrounded by hotels that are either a short walk or shuttle ride from the park. And most are a lot less expensive than the hotels on resort grounds. More often than not, I book my family into one of these Good Neighbor Hotels.

One of my favorites is the Anaheim Fairfield Inn by Marriott. It's a five-minute walk from Disneyland's main entrance. The rooms are simple, but clean and well appointed. The hotel doesn't have a complimentary continental breakfast, but there is a mini food court with a snack shop, coffee shop and a Pizza Hut Express. Nearby is Mimi's–a family-style restaurant that serves up a tasty breakfast and a McDonalds for fast, familiar fare.

Not much farther away is Howard Johnsons. Again, the rooms are standard, but comfortable. It's about an 8-minute walk from there to Disneyland's main entrance, but the real attraction of this hotel is its swimming pools and water play areas. Castaway Cove is a pirate-themed mini water park with water slides, a drench bucket, water cannons, a toddler wading pool and a Jacuzzi. For a more relaxed swim, head to the Garden Pool, which is surrounded by tall trees and blooming gardens.

Before booking any hotel outside the Disneyland Resort, check an online map to confirm the hotel is as close to the main entrance on Harbor Boulevard as possible. Many will say they're "right across the street from Disneyland" or have "Maingate" in their name, but that doesn't mean they're necessarily across the street from the entrance or anywhere near the Main Gate.

You'll also want to check the hotel's amenities list. Some offer complimentary continental breakfast, which can be a real time and money-saver. Not all offer in-room meal service, but for those that don't, restaurant delivery options are usually available.

Hotel/Resort Transportation

If you can't manage to book a hotel within the Disneyland Resort or within a few minutes' walk, don't worry. Most of the hotels surrounding the resort either have their own complimentary shuttle van or are on a public shuttle/bus route. If you're not sure whether your hotel offers a complimentary direct shuttle or access to the public system, ask the reservation desk to clarify.

If the hotel has its own shuttle van, the service is probably complimentary and a non-stop ride to and from the park. If you're taking one of the public shuttles, it will stop at other hotels on the way to and from the park. Daily or weekly passes for the public shuttles are usually available for purchase at the hotel front desk.

Whether you're taking a hotel or public shuttle, you'll want to plan your time accordingly. (That shuttle ride back can feel awfully long at night.) Also, during peak hours, vans and shuttles can fill up (meaning you have to wait for the next one), so expect some waiting and don't wait until you're drop-dead tired to head back to the hotel.

❤ Tear-Free Tip ❤

What happens if your child's cherished Disneyland balloon pops? No problem and no tears! Just return that busted balloon to any Disneyland Resort balloon vendor and they'll replace it – no charge!

Disneyland Dining

When and where you dine during your Disneyland vacation will depend on your family's eating habits, tastes and budget. Fortunately, you can choose from a variety of dining options in and around the Disneyland Resort. From award-winning gourmet restaurants to quick-serve cafés and all-you-can-eat buffets, there are virtually limitless levels of quality, flavor and service. In fact, there are so many choices, I could write a second book just on Disney dining (maybe a sequel?), but in the meantime, I'll limit this chapter to my very favorite restaurants plus some tips that I hope will prove helpful.

I usually plan one or two meals a day inside Disneyland Resort. It's convenient and it's fun to dine with a view of the parks. With over 70 dining and refreshment options, the hardest part about dining at Disneyland Park, Disney California Adventure, Downtown Disney District and their associated hotels is selecting the few places you'll have time to visit during your stay. Reservations are strongly recommended for any Disney full-service restaurant and can be made by calling Disney Dining at (714) 781-DINE. The prices that follow reflect reported dinner menu prices at the time of publication.

Dining in Disneyland Park

Blue Bayou (New Orleans Square)

Dine beneath sweeping willow branches and floating fireflies in the eternal twilight of the Pirates of the Caribbean bayou. The food is good but the atmosphere is the real treat in this dreamy escape from reality. Entrees like filet mignon, jambalaya and Cajun-spiced chicken are tasty, rich and satisfying. Kids can enjoy a baked chicken breast with pasta, seared salmon filet, mac & cheese or a small New York steak. For the best view, ask for a table by the rail (but expect a much longer wait for your table to be ready). Reservations recommended.

Adults: $29.99 – $46.99

Kids: $8.99 – $12.99

Big Thunder Ranch Barbecue (Frontierland)

Tucked into the woods behind Big Thunder Mountain Railroad, families are seated at gingham-clothed picnic tables and served an all-you-can-eat barbecue feast including chicken, ribs, corn on the cob, baked beans, coleslaw and corn bread. The food is terrific and worth saving up your appetite for. Plus, there's regularly scheduled live entertainment provided by Woody, Jessie, and Bullseye or a strolling cowboy troubadour. Reservations recommended.

Adults: $24.99

Kids: $9.99

Hungry Bear Restaurant (Critter Country)

This walk-up (counter service) restaurant has long been a favorite of mine because of its woodsy feel and second-story view of the Rivers of America as the Mark Twain

Riverboat chugs by. You can enjoy country favorites like fried chicken or fried green tomato sandwiches, plus sweet potato fries and tangy coleslaw. And don't forget to try the miniature blueberry pie! Kids' options include chicken nuggets, burgers or mac & cheese.
Adults: $8.69 – $10.69
Kids: $3.99 – $5.99

🐭 Tear-Free Tip 🐭

With the exception of food items for guests with specific dietary restrictions, food or beverage items are not permitted into either of the Disneyland Resort theme parks. That said, I know a lot of people who bring in food without incident. Still, I don't recommended bringing more than you really need for the time you'll be there.

Rancho del Zocalo Restaurante (Frontierland)
Festive outdoor dining and a great selection of Mexican food make this another Disneyland favorite. Choose from south-of-the-border favorites like grilled Mahi Mahi fish tacos, citrus fire-grilled chicken and fajita-style soft tacos. Bean and cheese burritos or chicken tacos will please most kids.
Adults: $9.99 – $13.49
Kids: $3.99 – $10.49

Gibson Girl Ice Cream Parlor (Main Street USA)
There's no shortage of sweet treats at Disneyland, but my family absolutely has to stop at this ice cream parlor at least once a visit. It's imbued with early American charm, and the ice cream is great (or maybe it just tastes better at Disneyland). My favorite has to be the Chocolate Chip Cookie Hot Fudge Sundae (comes with two freshly baked cookies – yum!). The sundaes are big enough to share for all but the biggest appetites (like mine). For even more fun, the parlor is connected to an old-fashioned penny arcade and candy shop.
Single scoop (cup, cone or dipped cone): $3.99 - $4.49
Double scoop (cup, cone or dipped cone): $4.49 - $5.19
Double scoop sundaes: $5.99 - $6.29

❦ Tear-Free Tip ❦

Downtown Disney District is a popular area with both park visitors and locals, so don't be surprised by large nighttime crowds and long wait times at the restaurants. Be sure to call ahead for reservations or plan to eat an hour or two before normal mealtimes.

Dining in Disney California Adventure

Disney California Adventure is gaining a well-earned reputation as a "foodies" amusement park. You'll find great character restaurants, fine dining options and better-than-average quick-service restaurants.

Another thing that some enjoy about dining at Disney California Adventure is that wine and beer are available at many of the restaurants (you won't find any alcohol at Disneyland Park).

If you decide to eat at one of the many quick-serve restaurants or haven't made reservations, plan to eat early. Lunch and dinner times can get pretty crowded and tend to run late. If you want to make sure you get seated during your preferred mealtime, stop by the restaurant or Guest Services in the morning to make reservations. You can also make reservations up to 60 days in advance by calling Disney Dining at (714) 781-DINE.

Ariel's Grotto (Paradise Pier)

The meals here are great, but the table-hopping princesses are what make this restaurant a family favorite. The meal starts as your table shares a generous antipasti tower, salads and fresh-baked breads. Adults select their entrée from Italian-American favorites including cioppino, grilled redfish, or pasta with Italian sausage while kids select from glazed skewered chicken, meatball lollipops, steak or pasta. Then your table shares a treat-filled platter for dessert. You can also make reservations that include a fixed-price meal and tickets to a Preferred Viewing section for the "World of Color" show. Reservations recommended.

(Prices include Preferred Viewing ticket.)
Adults: $36.99
Kids (3-9): $20.99

Carthay Circle Restaurant

It may be hard to decide which is more elegant, the food or the décor at the Carthay Circle Restaurant. The interior recalls the elegant beauty of the golden age of Hollywood while its menu features California-inspired cuisine. A rotating menu features entrees such as grilled quail stuffed with prosciutto-wrapped peaches, Colorado rack of lamb with fried zucchini blossoms or Sierra golden trout. A fresh fish selection, such as blue Belizean lemon fish with braised fennel, changes frequently. I've heard both fawning reviews and tales that the food was just so-so. But the wine selection, specialty cocktails and service always get high marks.

Appetizers: $11.00 – $16.00
Soup/Salad: $11.00
Entrees: $18.00 – $44.00 (Kids: $9.00 –$23.00)
Side Dish: $12.00

Napa Rose (Grand California Hotel & Spa)

For a fine dining experience, you probably can't beat Napa Rose. This award-winning restaurant has been rated as one of Orange County's very best by Zagat. Its rotating menu and extensive wine list has earned it accolades from Wine Spectator magazine, and its customer reviews are consistently glowing. Entrees like duck breast with apricot cashew puree or rolled flank steak with mushrooms are expertly prepared and delicious. Request a set at the Chef's Counter for a four-course prix fixe meal hand selected by the chef.

Appetizers: $13.00-$37.00
Soup/Salad: $12.00-$15.00
Entrees: $39.00 – $45.00 (Kids: $8.00 – $13.00)
Side Dish: $10.00 – $20.00
Dessert: $12.00 (Kids: $7.00 – $15.00)

Pacific Wharf Café (Pacific Wharf)

If you've worked up an appetite but don't feel like eating a big sit-down meal, this café will draw you with the smells of fresh-baked bread and flavorful soups. Our

favorite thing to do is to combine the two and order a steaming soup in a sourdough bread bowl. The broccoli and cheese soup and clam or corn chowders are all delicious options. Want something a little lighter? Choose one of their tasty sandwiches or salads.
Adults: $8.69 – $12.49
Kids: $5.99

🖤 Tear-Free Tip 🖤

If you're planning to see the "World of Color" show, you can pre-purchase a picnic meal online (http://disneyland. disney.go.com). Each meal (around $16) comes with a reserved viewing ticket for the show. Keep in mind that the section is reserved (there are no seats), so get to your designated area an hour before the show to stake out a good viewing spot.

Taste Pilots' Grill (Condor Flats)
Barbecue ribs, burgers (including chili, cheddar or blue cheese) and grilled chicken sandwiches are some of the tastiest options at this casual restaurant set inside an aviation hangar. My favorite part is the burger-toppings bar where you can customize your sandwich with fresh veggies and all your favorite fixings. You'll find the standard options for kids' meals – burgers, chicken nuggets and the ubiquitous mac & cheese.
Adults: $8.49 – $12.49
Kids: $2.99 – $6.49

❤ Tear-Free Tip ❤

If you book your trip through the Walt Disney Travel Company, you can simplify meal planning by purchasing a Disney Dining Plan. For a simple per-person fee, you choose the number of meals and snacks per day and then use Disneyland Resort vouchers at dining locations throughout the Disneyland Resort. Some limitations and regular reservation recommendations apply.

Wine Country Trattoria at the Golden Vine Winery (Pacific Warf)

This could be my favorite place to dine in the entire Disneyland Resort. On nice days, ask for outdoor seating and enjoy sunny Italian fare like roasted vegetable panini, lasagna and shrimp scampi. For kids, they have meatball or grilled cheese sandwiches or grilled chicken with pasta. This restaurant's fresh, light fare, dappled sunlight (and a glass of California Cab-Merlot for me) makes this a wonderful lunch spot.

Adults: $13.49 – $20.49

Kids: $7.99 – $8.99

Dining in Downtown Disney District

Within the huge shopping, entertainment and dining concourse between Disneyland Park and Disney California Adventure, you'll find over 16 dining destinations, including large sit-down restaurants as well as more intimate options.

You may already be familiar with some of the restaurants such as Rainforest Café, House of Blues or ESPN Zone. Others, like Ralph Brennan's Jazz Kitchen, Tortilla Jo's and Naples Ristorante e Pizzeria offer a variety of fare, entertainment options and even live music.

One of our favorite spots is Uva Bar–an al fresco dining experience in the heart of Downtown Disney District. It's a great place to grab a cool drink and some appetizers or a light salad and enjoy the sounds of live music and the bustle of Downtown Disney.

The recently added Earl of Sandwich is a popular spot for hearty sandwiches on fresh baked bread.

Dining Outside the Resort

Unless we scheduled a Disney Character Breakfast inside the resort, I almost always plan to eat breakfast at our hotel. Some hotels provide a complimentary breakfast buffet (muffins, pastries, cereals, fruit, waffles, etc.). When we stay at one of these, I usually get up early, head down to the buffet and grab a few options to bring back to the room for the family to enjoy. It's a lot easier than trying to get the whole family down to the buffet, fight the crowd, wrangle a table, help everyone select their meals and eat in anything resembling a relaxing manner.

Since we often take a break from the park around midday, we often have lunch at the hotel or a nearby restaurant. As much fun as the parks are, it can be a relief to get away from the crowds and just relax by the pool with a light lunch, or to order something from room service and eat after a long nap.

For dinner, the streets surrounding Disneyland Resort are chock-a-block with eateries. There are plenty of familiar "faces" (Denny's, McDonalds, Tony Roma's, IHop, Ruth's Chris Steakhouse, Carl's Jr., Taco Bell, Quizno's), which can feel like a welcome "taste of home" when you're on the road. Don't be surprised if some of their menu items are a little higher priced than you're used to. Still, a meal at one of these restaurants can save you a chunk of change compared to dining in the parks.

Preparing Your Child

There are many ways to mentally prepare your child for a trip to Disneyland. Besides discussing rules and expected behavior (and other "parenty" stuff), you can also have a lot of fun getting him or her pumped up and excited for the trip.

Know the Disney Characters

The more Disney characters your child knows, the more exciting it will be to see them in person. And many of the rides are themed specifically to re-tell the classic tales. Has your child ever seen an original Mickey Mouse cartoon, "Peter Pan" or "Cinderella"? Characters from classic Disney animated movies and Pixar films are well represented at Disneyland Resort. Not old enough for some of these movies? Check out some Disney storybooks from your local library and introduce them during bedtime stories.

Talk About Behavior

Letting your kids know your expectations for their behavior during any trip is a good idea. You probably have rules for when you visit the mall or grocery store, the same should be true while on vacation. This doesn't need to be a big talk or a lecture. Just impress upon them some "Disneyland Do's and Don'ts." For instance:

Do:
- Wear sunscreen every day
- Be patient in lines
- Let us know if you get tired
- Say please and thank you
- Be kind to Cast Members
- Stay where we can see you
- Eat the food you order
- Cooperate and compromise

Don't:
- Wander off or run ahead
- Push or shove people
- Fuss at naptime
- Keep asking if the answer is "no"
- Tug on or hit Disney Characters
- Panic if you get lost or separated
- Climb on rails or rocks while in line
- Forget your hat and sunglasses

Manage Expectations

Remember, as magical a place as Disneyland seems, no actual magic takes place. Wishing won't make a temporarily closed ride reopen, and weather can unexpectedly interrupt events like fireworks and parades. In short, don't make promises you cannot personally keep.

If you don't have control over where and when Cinderella (or whoever) appears, don't make a big buildup about seeing her. That goes for all events, attractions and characters unless you've confirmed their availability.

Speaking of attractions, it's important to have a clear understanding of which rides your children are tall enough to go on. Trust me, you don't want to spend 20 or 30 minutes in line for a ride only to be turned away – and if they don't meet the minimum height, that is what will happen. That's why it's a good idea to measure your child prior to your trip and reference the ride height guide on page 137. You'll save a lot of time and tears when you know which Disneyland Resort attractions they are tall enough to ride now and which ones they can look forward to in the future.

Get Them Excited

Some parents like to surprise their kids and tell them they're going to Disneyland on the day they leave or even when they're at the airport. If your child has been begging to go, this is sure to raise an enthusiastic response (cover your ears!).

Other parents like to let the excitement build over time. A great way to do this is with a countdown calendar. This could be as simple as circling the big day on the calendar and then marking off each day with a big "X." It could be as involved as creating something like an Advent calendar with a little gift or treat inside for them to open each day. If you go this route, you can kill two birds with one stone and make the gifts items they'll use on the trip like sunglasses, an autograph book, a coloring book or other diversions for the airplane.

Get Them Involved

A great way to get kids prepared for a trip is to let them help in the research, scheduling and preparation. Unless you want the trip to be a surprise, why not let them help select the best time to go, what day to start packing and what things to bring. You can even discuss the budget and how it will be broken down into meals, hotel, airfare, park tickets, etc. On a smaller scale, you can discuss your child's spending allowance for the trip and strategies to make the money last.

If your kids are too young (or not interested) in that kind of involvement, you can keep it simple and view Disneyland Resort maps or a vacation planning DVD (available free from the Disneyland website). You can talk about the attractions, parades and events each family member would like to do and then plan how your day will go.

Plan for Waiting in Lines

Unlike other amusement parks, the lines at Disneyland are an immersive experience in and of themselves. Many of them use design, décor and props to tell an introductory story to the ride guests are about to embark upon. Still, even the most entertaining lines can be a challenge for small children. Having a plan to help keep them entertained can make life easier for everyone.

• Pack a "fun kit" for kids to carry on their back. Fill it with reading and activity books, small toys and games.

• If you have an iPhone, the app "Lots To Do In Line: Disneyland" offers visual scavenger hunts and trivia questions for each ride and land in the resort. ($5.99 on iTunes.)

• If a Cast Member is nearby, ask if they know any interesting stories about the ride you're waiting in line for. Generally, they're very knowledgeable and happy to share what they know.

• Send pictures, emails or text messages to family and share stories about your trip so far.

• Look for Hidden Mickeys. You'll find them all over

the park and in many attraction lines. They are some-times tricky to spot, but cast members are happy to give you hints.

• Play "road" games like I-Spy, 20 Questions or take turns asking each other Disney trivia questions.

Safety First

Even with the best planning, unexpected things do sometimes happen. So it's important for you and your kids to know what to do in those situations.

Explain that if you become separated from one an-other, they should not go looking for you – you will find them. Tell them it's okay to ask one of the Disney Cast Members (wearing a Disneyland employee badge) for assistance. They'll be taken to the Child Care Cen-ter where they'll be reunited with you. To speed up the process, make your child a "My Parents" card featuring both parents' names, cell phone numbers and photos on it. You can have this card laminated and attached, like a luggage tag, to their belt loop or lanyard if they're wear-ing one. There are also a number of web sites that offer custom temporary tattoos. Order some with your cell phone number and apply to your child's wrist in the morning.

If you have older children along and they're old enough to explore the park on their own, but don't have a cell phone, have them keep in touch with you via walkie-talkie. You can purchase a pair online for as little as $20.

Some children get very upset if they get even a mi-nor boo-boo. This distress can be caused by fear of the unknown. (How long will it hurt? What do I do? Does this mean I have to go home?) If this reaction is typical for your child, you can let him or her know in advance that if he or she falls or gets hurt, there's nothing to worry about. If needed, there's a First Aid station where boo-boos get bandaged and you'll be able to get back to the fun in no time.

 Tear-Free Tip

For one weekend each October, Disneyland becomes home to the unofficial "Gay Days" celebration. Hundreds of LGBT guests, their children, family and supporters wear red t-shirts and enjoy the resort united in community. Disneyland hotels are frequently sold out for this popular event.

Money-Saving Tips

One rumor many people hear about Disneyland is that it is ex-pen-sive. Well, I can't say I really disagree with that assessment. For example, to get 3-day park-hopper tickets for 2 adults and 2 children, you can expect to pay around $900. Not exactly chicken feed. Then, when you add in airfare, ground transportation, hotel, meals and souvenirs... ouch.

But, don't let that dissuade you. With just a little time and effort, you can save money on everything from hotel rooms to park tickets.

Check for Discount Park Tickets

I've seen discounted Disneyland Resort tickets at Costco, Safeway and offered by hotels. Just keep your eyes open (or search online) and compare those prices to the ones offered at the Disneyland website (which will be the same at the gate). If you do purchase tickets on-line, be sure to do so only from a trusted, reliable source (like the official Disney website). I don't recommend purchasing park tickets on eBay or Craigslist or from anyone you don't personally know and trust implicitly. There's a possibility the tickets could be forgeries or duplicates. And that won't save you any money at all.

Find a Great Travel Agent

I've booked plenty of Disneyland trips on my own. I've also used travel agents on many occasions to book my family's Disneyland vacation. Besides saving you a lot of time researching and comparing prices, a travel agent (especially one that specializes in Disneyland vacations) can look for bargains and special deals that you might not be able to find. They can also usually retroactively apply discounts if better fares or offers come up after the time of your booking. Some even provide little extras or make special arrangements that make your trip extra special. And once your trip is booked, everything you need–from airplane tickets and hotel information to ground transportation and park tickets–comes carefully organized in an easy-to-use kit.

Your agent will also work with you to maximize your budget. Are you willing to make a connecting flight to save a few hundred dollars on airfare? Let your agent know. Willing to travel farther to the park so you and the kids can have connecting hotel rooms? Tell them. Willing to visit Disneyland when the rates are lower? Be sure to mention that too.

The best part about working with an agent is it won't add any cost to your trip – they're compensated by hotel, airline and vacation industries.

Ask for Discounts

Do you have a AAA card? Are you over 55? Are you a veteran, student or member of Costco? When it comes time to book your airfare, hotel and what-have-you, be sure to ask about any discounts you can use. I've found that most of the people who take reservations almost never ask, so it's up to you to ask for the discount.

Drink Up

A bottle of water can cost $2 to $3 inside the parks. Some folks buy bottled water outside the park, freeze it the night before and then store the bottle in a rental locker (maybe with a few snacks). We usually just bring one aluminum bottle of water inside the park and then refill it for free from any of the many water fountains or at restaurants around the park. I also like the refill plan because it reduces waste.

Check Again

Months after booking her trip with Disney, a friend of mine had the idea of checking to see if the rates had gone down. As luck would have it, Disney was having a 25% off promotion. Despite the fact that she had to pay a $50 penalty to change her reservation, the amount she saved on her hotel more than made up for it.

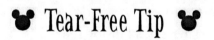

❤ Tear-Free Tip ❤

Pretty much every shop and restaurant at the park takes credit and debit cards, so it can be easy to lose track of how much money you spend. If you need to stick to a hard and fast budget, bring that day's allowance in cash.

Pack a Snack

To help avoid spending a lot of money on sugary between-meal snacks, plan ahead and pack a small, soft-sided bag with portable, healthy options. Our favorites are granola bars, Fig Newtons, goldfish crackers and nuts. If you have an insulated bag, consider adding cheese sticks, carrot sticks, apple slices and juice boxes. If you don't have a stroller to help carry these items, rent a locker and retrieve the bag before hunger pangs set in.

Pre-Shop

Some people (though I'm not one) purchase souvenirs (stuffed animals, t-shirts, autograph books, toys, etc.) prior to visiting Disneyland at their neighborhood department store or toy store. They purchase them on sale, hide them in their bag and then give them as surprise gifts at the beginning or end of a Disneyland day. The idea being, it satisfies their kids' desire for souvenirs and keeps them from starting up the "I-want-it I-want-it I-want-it" chant.

Eat Out(side the Parks)

For a hungry family of four, it's easy to spend $80 to $100 on a single meal inside the parks. By eating just one meal a day outside the parks, it's easy to save hundreds during your trip. With the money we save eating outside the park, we feel good about splurging for one of Disneyland's more expensive restaurants.

And if you want to skip paying for one meal a day, be sure to stay at a hotel that offers a complimentary continental breakfast. They're typically not fancy (cereals, pastries, maybe some waffles) but they're filling and the price sure is right.

Control the Collectibles

With so many irresistible shops and souvenir items at Disneyland Resort, you could spend a small fortune on character-themed clothes, toys, figurines, stuffed animals, jewelry, costumes, even housewares, fine crystal and vacation property. My recommendation? Choose a souvenir budget for each family member and stick to it. If the kids are old enough to handle money, you could give them Disney Dollars or gift cards, which are available at the ticket kiosk and many Disneyland Resort shops.

Another plan is to announce to the family that all souvenir purchases will be done on the last day. Tell them the maximum amount they can spend and be ready to help them make the tough choices. This way, each person can have fun window shopping, looking for that one or two items he or she really wants to buy. Of course, the best souvenirs are the photos and memories you'll collect on the trip. Just remember that, and you'll be fine.

Skip the Car

Unless you really need your own wheels, don't bother renting a car. We usually just take a cab to and from the airport (about $40 + tip from Santa Ana) and use public transportation to the park if it's too far to walk. The exception is when we plan on seeing a lot of other sights besides Disneyland. On one trip, we managed to pack in 3 days at Disneyland plus a couple of days at Universal Studios, Hollywood, Venice Beach and more. That time, a car really came in handy. If you think you might need a car for just part of your trip, see if your hotel has a rental car available on premises.

Stock Your Room

Some of the hotels we've stayed at near Disneyland come with a mini-fridge, microwave and coffee maker. When it does, we pop down to a nearby grocery store and stock up on milk, cereal, fruit and beverages. You can eat a fast, convenient breakfast or lunch in your room or pop some popcorn for an in-room movie. Besides, it'll help avoid those expensive vending machine prices.

Trade Up

If you're a collector of Disney items, you might enjoy Pin Trading. You'll see people all over the park with pins honoring characters, holidays and special events. Part of the fun is seeing if people want to trade pins with you. Even better is that any Disney Cast Member wearing pins will gladly make a trade with you. That's why it's a good idea to have a few basic (i.e., lower-priced) pins to trade for other, fancier pins.

Don't Get Caught in the Cold

If you visit Disneyland during the cooler, wetter months, plan ahead and pack clothes that will keep you warm and dry. You can purchase an easy-to-pack travel poncho on an online site like Amazon for $3 to $5. If you have to buy one at the park, expect to pay $8 to $15. I'm not a fan of ponchos, so I prefer to bring a waterproof jacket and baseball cap.

Make Purposeful Purchases

Souvenirs don't have to be toys, candy or gifts, they can also be useful items. Character-festooned sunglasses, hats and jackets can be worn again and again. They can also come in handy while you're at the park. For instance, when a hot summer day turns into a chilly evening, my family heads to a Disneyland shop to pick up sweatshirts. We stay warm while waiting for the fireworks and we each have a fun keepsake.

Tear-Free Tip

Service animals are welcome in most locations of Disneyland Resort. Keep in mind that service animals will need to remain on a leash or harness at all times and that Cast Members are not allowed to handle service animals.

Special Services

It doesn't take many trips to Disneyland before you begin to see that it's the people – the Cast Members – that help make it the magical and special destination it is. When I first started going, I was loath to ask for directions or help from Cast Members (typical man, right?). But, as I soon learned, they are genuinely eager to help in any way they can. Now I don't hesitate to ask questions about the park, its history, the attractions, or even just talk to them.

Guest Relations

Found inside City Hall in Disneyland Park and just inside the entrance to Disney California Adventure, Guest Relations is the perfect place to stop, ask questions, get directions or make dining reservations. You may have to wait in line, but the service is personable and very helpful.

Lost & Found

Did someone drop his or her teddy bear? Can't find your favorite hoodie? Leave your video camera behind? There is now a single Lost & Found center for all personal items lost inside Disneyland Park, Disney California Adventure and Downtown Disney District. You'll find it just outside the main entrance to California Adventure.

Lost Children

If one of your party goes missing, don't panic. Just contact any Disney Cast Member or visit the nearest Baby Care Center, and someone will be on hand to assist you. Lost children are taken to the nearest Baby Care Center to be reunited with their parents or guardian. Note: There is no Baby Care Center in Downtown Disney District. Lost children found in the Downtown Disney District will be taken to the Baby Care Center in Disneyland Park.

Infant Needs

Disneyland Resort offers special Baby Care Centers where parents can go for a quiet and private place to nurse, feed and change their baby (though most if not all restrooms have changing stations). I've never taken advantage of these centers myself, but the positive online comments I've read make them sound like a great convenience for parents. Disneyland Park's Baby Care Center is located on the far end of Main Street, U.S.A. and Disney California Adventure has one in its Pacific Wharf section.

First Aid

Need to bandage a boo-boo? Does Mommy have a headache? You'll find a First Aid station staffed with a nurse to help. On one trip, a friend ate something with orange peel (she's allergic), and the nurse there was very helpful with an analgesic and a genial, calming manner.

Guided Tours

Do you want to get the most out of your Disneyland trip or just need an insider to show you around? Disneyland Resort offers a variety of tours. From a historical tour detailing how Walt Disney wove his personal history, philosophy and imagination into the park to adventuresome treasure hunts, there are guided tours for a variety of interests and budgets.

I was lucky enough to be able to experience a personal 8-hour VIP Tour. The guide was charming, friendly, and gave us a customized and amazing day. She was our personal FASTPASS, taking us right into the FASTPASS line for many attractions. On many attractions that didn't have a FASTPASS line, she was able to take us through the exit to the front of the line. She also made all our meal reservations and secured VIP seating for both "Fantasmic!" and "World of Color." Yes, for one sweet day, we were that family that all the other guests hate. There's no question that the VIP Tour is costly, but it is a truly magical way to experience Disneyland.

For more information, visit the Disneyland web site and click the tours link under the Parks & Hotels banner at the bottom or call (714) 781-8687 up to one month in advance of your visit.

For Guests With Special Needs

One of the amazing things about Disneyland is that you'll see kids with a wide variety of abilities enjoying the park. Every kid's smile is magical, and it's nice to know that Disney works to make sure it meets the needs of the widest variety of people possible. Will every child be able to ride every attraction? No – but that's true for all kids. Still, parents of kids with developmental, sensory or mobility limitations will find Disneyland Resort a welcoming and accommodating place. But like all adventures, it takes a little extra planning.

I'm by no means an expert on travel planning for kids with special needs, but I want to make sure that parents are aware that these services are available. For a complete list of services, review the Disabilities section under Guest Services of the official Disneyland website.

Wheelchair and ECV Accessibility

If a guest with limited mobility is able to transfer out of their wheelchair or electric conveyance vehicle (ECV), he or she will have access to the majority of attractions at Disneyland Park and Disney California Adventure. Be advised that he or she will need to be able to complete the transfer alone or with the help of people in their party (Cast Members are not allowed to assist in transfer). If he or she cannot safely transfer, many attractions can be enjoyed while remaining in a wheelchair.

A few attractions (Finding Nemo Submarine Voyage and Sleeping Beauty Castle Walkthrough) have wheelchair-accessible alternative experiences. In addition, guests may remain in their wheelchair or ECV for the following attractions:

Disneyland Park

- Big Thunder Ranch
- Buzz Lightyear Astro Blasters (EVC transfer to wheelchair required)
- Captain EO Starring Michael Jackson
- Disneyland Monorail
- Disneyland Story presenting Great Moments with Mr. Lincoln

- Disneyland Railroad (New Orleans Square, Mickey's Toontown and Tomorrowland stations)
- Enchanted Tiki Room
- Finding Nemo Submarine Voyage (Alternative experience)
- Frontierland Shootin' Gallery
- Goofy's Playhouse
- Innoventions
- "it's a small world" (EVC transfer to wheelchair required)
- Jungle Cruise
- King Arthur Carrousel
- Little Mermaid – Ariel's Undersea Adventure (EVC transfer to wheelchair required)
- Main Street Cinema
- Mark Twain Riverboat
- Many Adventures of Winnie the Pooh (EVC transfer to wheelchair required)
- Mickey's House and Meet Mickey
- Minnie's House
- Pirate's Lair on Tom Sawyer Island
- Pixie Hollow
- Rapunzel and Flynn Rider
- Sleeping Beauty Castle Walkthrough (Alternative experience)
- Starcade (Video Game Arcade)

Disney California Adventure
- Bakery Tour
- Disney Animation
- Disney Junior – Live On Stage!
- Disney's Aladdin – A Musical Spectacular
- Duffy the Disney Bear
- Games of the Boardwalk

- It's Tough to Be a Bug!
- King Triton's Carousel
- Mickey's Fun Wheel (EVC transfer to wheelchair required)
- Monsters Inc. Mike & Sulley to the Rescue! (EVC transfer to wheelchair required)
- Muppet*Vision 3D
- Princess Dot Puddle Park
- Radiator Springs Racers
- Redwood Creek Challenge Trail (certain challenges only)
- Toy Story Mania! (EVC transfer to wheelchair required)
- Turtle Talk with Crush
- Walt Disney Imagineering Blue Sky Cellar
- World of Color show

All restaurants within the Disneyland Resort are wheelchair accessible.

Service Animals

Service animals are welcome in most locations of Disneyland Resort. Keep in mind that service animals will need to remain on a leash or harness at all times and it is requested that you allow your dog to relieve itself only in designated areas. If you wish to ride an attraction that a service animal is not allowed on, you will need someone in your party to wait with the animal. You can then switch places and wait with the service animal while they ride.

Hearing Disability Services

Disneyland provides several options to assist with hearing disabilities. An Assisted Listening, Handheld

Captioning or Reflective Captioning device is provided for use on many attractions and shows, free of charge (a refundable $25 deposit is required). These are recommended for guests with mild to moderate hearing loss. Written aids are also available for several attractions and shows.

Disneyland also provides Sign Language Interpretation for live shows on alternating days. (Disneyland Park: Saturdays and Mondays. Disney California Adventure: Fridays and Sundays.) It's recommended that you call 7 days in advance to confirm shows, dates, times and availability of Sign Language Interpretation. (714) 781-6176 for voice or (714) 781-7292 for TTY.

Sensory Sensitivities

Guests with sensitivity issues, including photosensitivity and seizure disorders, may have a particularly challenging time enjoying Disneyland Resort. From strobe lights to loud sounds and a cacophony of odors, there is no shortage of stimulation. The Disneyland website recommends checking with your personal physician for specific instructions prior to your visit.

Developmental Disabilities

Because there are so many variations and degrees of developmental disabilities, it's best to contact Disneyland Guest Relations to discuss your family member's particular situation and, if necessary, come up with a plan of action. One friend of mine, whose son has Asperger's Syndrome, knew that her son would be incapable of waiting in line for attractions. She was justifiably concerned that this might mean Disneyland wasn't a vacation option for her family. Guest Relation's solution was a complimentary Guest Assistance Card that allowed her son (and those with him) to ride on attractions without having to wait in line. Your family's solution may be different, but my friend convinced me that Guest Relations representatives take each family's situation seriously and work hard to address guest's concerns. You can speak to a live Guest Relations representative by calling (714) 781-7290 from 7:00 a.m. to 6:00 p.m. PST daily.

Food Allergies and Special Requests

Most Disney Resort restaurants offer vegetarian, low-fat, reduced sodium and no-sugar added items. However, these items might not be obvious on the menu, so ask your server for more details.

Guests with food allergies or special dietary requirements may have a more challenging time. Your best bet is to stick to Disneyland Resort's table-service restaurants (the kind that accept reservations). These facilities can accommodate most food allergies or intolerances including:

• Gluten or wheat
• Shellfish
• Soy
• Lactose or dairy
• Peanuts and tree nuts
• Fish
• Eggs
• Corn

The servers and chefs at table-service restaurants are used to questions regarding food allergies, so don't be shy about asking. Keep in mind that the restaurant staff will do their best to accommodate guests with dietary requirements, but they cannot guarantee that they can meet every request. Guests with special dietary needs are allowed to bring their own food into any of the Disneyland Resort parks or restaurants.

If you would like to purchase a kosher meal at a Disneyland Resort restaurant, you'll need to request one 24 hours in advance by calling (714) 781-DINE.

If you book your trip through the Walt Disney Travel Company, you can simplify meal planning by purchasing a Disney Dining Plan. For a simple per-person fee, you choose the number of meals and snacks per day and then use Disneyland Resort vouchers at dining locations throughout the Disneyland Resort. Some limitations and regular reservation recommendations apply.

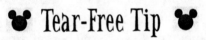

Tear-Free Tip

If you need a little caffeine to get you
through your day but are particular
about your coffee, Disneyland Resort
now has two Starbucks inside the parks.
In Disneyland Park, visit Market House
on Main Street, U.S.A. In Disney California Adventure, visit Fiddler, Fifer and
Practical Cafe at the end of Buena Vista
Street. Don't be surprised by crazy-long
lines in the mornings; the counters are
well-staffed and the service is speedy.

Fun Finds

Part of the fun of Disneyland is learning more about the history, myths and mysteries swirling around the legendary park. Over the last 50 years, much about the resort has changed, but wherever you visit, there's an interesting tidbit of trivia just waiting to be discovered.

There are many books dedicated to the history and mythology surrounding Disneyland, so I'll just share a few of my favorite finds here.

Walt's Home Away From Home

As you first step into Disneyland and onto Main Street, U.S.A., one of your first sights will be the Disneyland Fire Station. What many people don't know is that Walt Disney himself often stayed in a small apartment on the second floor during construction of the park. It's still furnished, but sadly is not open to the public. In Walt's memory, a lamp remains lit in the apartment window. The fire station is also the only building on Main Street, U.S.A. that has a full-sized second floor. If you look carefully, the rest of the buildings are built using forced perspective (with a smaller second floor) to make them appear taller than they really are.

It All Started With a Mouse

If your kids only know Mickey Mouse from his current Disney Junior incarnation, you can give them a brief and entertaining history lesson at the Main Street Cinema. Inside, you can watch clips from several classic Mickey cartoons including "Steamboat Willie" – the first sync sound cartoon and the first Mickey Mouse Cartoon released (two cartoons, "Plane Crazy" and "Gallopin' Goucho" were produced first but released later). It's also a great place to escape the noise and bustle of the park for a few minutes.

Magical Moment

A little further down Main Street, U.S.A., you'll find Main Street Magic Shop. It carries a wide variety of easy-to-learn magic tricks and jokes. (It's also where, once upon a time, future funnyman Steve Martin worked as a teenager.) Stop inside, the Cast Member there will be more than happy to demonstrate a few mind-boggling magic tricks (all available for purchase, of course).

Hidden Mickeys

Throughout the park, keep your eyes peeled for "Hidden Mickeys." A Hidden Mickey is (most frequently) that classic three circle silhouette, which can be found painted onto signs, designed into attractions, formed with rocks or other background objects – even embedded in pathways. Many are deliberately placed around the park, but it's easy to see how they can occur naturally too. It's like a treasure hunt that can be played anywhere in the resort. (If you want a little help, Hidden Mickey guidebooks are available.)

Historic Animatronics

Many of Disneyland's most popular attractions feature Audio-Animatronics – those moving, singing, talking electronic figures. To see the very first animatronic show ever created, head to the Enchanted Tiki Room. The show, virtually unchanged since its 1963 premier, is still a charmer.

Great Moments with Mr. Lincoln, a stirring tribute to American history, was originally created for the State of Illinois pavilion for the 1964 New York World's Fair. For the same World's Fair, Disney also created a special exhibit for Pepsi and UNICEF – it's still one of Disneyland's most popular attractions – "it's a small world."

Disneyland's Past

Since its opening day, Disneyland has never stopped evolving and changing. While many attractions are but a distant memory, some have left behind mementos. One of the most curious of these is Disneyland's Indian Village.

When Disneyland opened in 1955, America was still enjoying its fascination with the "Old West" – or at least the 1950s vision of the Old West. Along with a stagecoach or pack mule ride through a western wilderness, you could also visit a reproduction of a Plains Indian village. Guests were invited to see craftwork demonstrations, peek inside a teepee and meet an Indian Chief.

Its sanitized and one-sided view of history would make such an attraction objectionable by today's cultural standards, but it epitomized America's nostalgic love for a time that never was. Though the village closed in 1971, its memory lingers in its last remaining attraction, Davy Crocket Explorer Canoes.

Movie Memorabilia

Many of Disneyland's attractions are based on motion pictures (and vice versa) so it's not surprising that hidden in some of the attractions are actual movie props.

Perhaps most notable is the stone treasure chest from the first "Pirates of the Caribbean" movie. Keep a sharp eye, and there you'll see it, full of cursed pirate gold, inside the Pirates of the Caribbean attraction.

In the ghostly party scene of the Haunted Mansion, you'll see the pipe organ originally played by Captain Nemo in Disney's "20,000 Leagues Under the Sea."

While waiting in line for Indiana Jones Adventure, look for a Mercedes-Benz truck that is reportedly from "Raiders of the Lost Ark." Note the missing hood ornament Harrison Ford's character snapped off while dangling from the front of the truck.

Disneyland Dream Suite

Just above the Pirates of the Caribbean is the Disneyland Dream Suite. It was originally built to be a luxurious apartment where Walt could entertain investors and important visitors. In fact, if you look at the balcony, you can still see Walt and Roy Disney's (Walt's brother and business partner) initials in the iron rail. When Walt passed away, the uncompleted project was shelved.

Years later, I had the pleasure of touring the space while it was open to the public as an art gallery. Then, for the Year of a Million Dreams celebration, it was renovated with many of the apartment's original design elements to become the 2,200 square-foot Disneyland Dream Suite. It is reserved as a prize for specific promotions and is not available to be reserved by the general public.

Club 33

Wander down the street from the Dream Suite and you'll see a simple "33" etched in glass next to a nondescript door. This is the entrance to Club 33, the most exclusive club in Disneyland. Only members and their guests may ride the private elevator up to a dining club featuring a five-star restaurant and cocktail lounge. Its members and guests are wealthy executives, government officials, foreign dignitaries and celebrities. Rumor has it that the waiting list to join has grown so long that they no longer add people to the list. I don't expect I'll ever see the inside for myself (I've seen photos online), but I can dream, can't I?

Silhouette Studio

In an easy-to-overlook shop on Main Street, U.S.A. sits a little silhouette portrait studio. Honestly, the first time I saw this place, I thought it was just another charming turn-of-the-century façade. But this little shop hides a very big talent. Using just a pair of small scissors and a keen eye, a Cast Member will deftly create a hand-cut silhouette of your kids, yourself or your whole family. No photography, computers or tricks used – just hands and talent.

It's very interesting to watch these mini masterpieces being created, and the keepsake is a truly unique memory from the park. You get two copies for under $10 and can get a frame for just a little more. Hang one on the wall and place the other in your Disneyland scrapbook (or send it as a souvenir to the grandparents).

Go Princess

Once you are through the entrance of Sleeping Beauty Castle, you'll soon see the Bibbidi Bobbidi Boutique. This princess-themed beauty salon not only sells costumes, but also gives girls sparkly hairdos, glittery (child-appropriate) makeup and face painting. They do offer pirate-themed options for boys, but they're also great about accommodating your child's particular preferences.

Happy Birthday

I can't imagine a better place to celebrate a birthday than Disneyland Resort. If your kid is lucky enough to be there on or near his or her birthday, be sure to pick up a complimentary Happy Birthday button at City Hall in Disneyland Park or at Guest Services in Disney California Adventure. Cast Members will be saying, "Happy Birthday" all day long, making your child feel extra special. Any of the restaurants (especially the Character Breakfasts) are great for a birthday meal, and you can even purchase a small birthday cake at one of the bakeries at the resort (they come in Princess or Pirate themes and include a keepsake treasure chest).

Celebrate the Seasons

Every town has its own way of celebrating the holidays, but I respectfully submit that no one celebrates the holidays as joyfully and magically as Disneyland Resort. Whether you're planning to visit during Halloween, Christmas, Thanksgiving or the Fourth of July, expect special parades, fireworks, decorations and events. For instance, during October (which Disney calls Halloweentime), one of the parks closes early on certain nights of the week for Mickey's Halloween Party. The park is dotted with kid-centric dance parties and trick-or-treat stations. And everyone (grown ups too!) get to dress up in costumes. Special tickets are required ($49–$64) for Mickey's Halloween Party, but we found it well worth the added cost.

Some of the rides even get special holiday treatment. During Halloweentime, Space Mountain becomes Ghost Galaxy at Space Mountain with supernatural scenes and menacing music. And from October to New Years' Jack Skellington from "Tim Burton's The Nightmare Before Christmas" takes over the Haunted Mansion and re-dresses it in a crazy collision between Christmas and Halloween. For December, "it's a small world" also gets even jollier with holiday costumes, decorations and music.

Consumption with a Conscience

When you consider the number of guests served at Disneyland Resort, it's hard not to ponder just how much pollution and waste are created every day. While I don't have the figures for that (though I'm sure it's plenty) I do know about some of the resort's green initiatives that may help ease your conscience. For instance, when you're riding the steam-powered Disneyland Railroad or any of the motorized vehicles on Main Street, U.S.A., you may be glad to know that they're all powered by clean-burning biodiesel fuel. Similarly, when Disney revamped the submarine ride, it switched from diesel engines to electric.

And though there are recycling bins all over the park, you can rest assured that the regular garbage bins are also gone through to make sure that recyclable materials don't end up in landfills. But what about all the smoke created from the nightly fireworks spectaculars? Disney managed to greatly reduce that too by shooting the fireworks into the sky with compressed air instead of smoke-emitting rockets.

Talk to the Animals

Behind Thunder Mountain you'll find Big Thunder Ranch – a charming petting zoo where kids can come face-to-snout with a bevy of barnyard animals. There's a small barn where kids can see and touch cows, goats, donkeys and pigs.

If you're there around Thanksgiving, you just might see the turkey that got pardoned from the White House. During the winter holidays, the barnyard becomes home to a herd of reindeer. I wonder whom those could belong to? If you need a hint, look for a jolly man in red in the holiday parade.

And speaking of animals, the horses employed at Disneyland are impressive in their size, beauty and temperament. After years of training to prepare them for the noise, balloons, kids and excitement in the park, they begin their jobs. They work between one and four hours a day – two days on, then two days off. During their days off, they're lovingly cared for at the Circle D Corral (off limits to guests, sadly) where they rest, play and are exercised by a group of vets and grooms.

Useful Sites & Numbers

Alaska Airlines
http://www.alaskaair.com
Ask about their annual Kids Fly Free to Disneyland promotion

Anaheim Resort Transit
http://www.rideart.org
(714) 563-5287

California Tourism
http://www.visitcalifornia.com

Disneyland Disabilities Overview
http://disneyland.disney.go.com/plan/guest-services/guests-with-disabilities

Disneyland Resort Dining
http://disneyland.disney.go.com/dining
(714) 781- DINE (3463)

Disneyland Resort Hotels
(714) 956-MICKEY (6425)

Disneyland Tours
http://disneyland.disney.go.com/tours
(714) 781-4565

Food Allergies/Dietary Requests
http://disneyland.disney.go.com/plan/guest-services/special-dietary-requests

Free Disney Vacation Planning DVD
http://www.disneyvacations.com/dv/en_US/VacationPlanningDVD

Frequently Asked Questions
http://disneyland.disney.go.com/faq

Guest Information (Recorded)
(714) 781-4565

Guest Services
http://disneyland.disney.go.com/plan/guest-services

Height Requirements
http://disneyland.disney.go.com/plan/guest-services/height-requirements

Hotels Near Disneyland
http://disneyland.disney.go.com/hotels/good-neighbor

Kennel Services
http://disneyland.disney.go.com/plan/guest-services/kennel
(714) 781-7290

Los Angeles Airport
http://www.lawa.org/welcomelax.aspx

Mobile Apps
http://disneyland.disney.go.com/plan/guest-services/mobile-apps

Orange County (John Wayne) Airport
http://www.ocair.com/

Park Hours and Schedule
http://disneyland.disney.go.com/calendar/daily

Resort Maps
http://disneyland.disney.go.com/maps

Resort Overview
http://disneyland.disney.go.com

Sign language interpretation
(714) 781-6176 for voice (714) 781-7292 for TTY

Stroller Rental
http://disneyland.disney.go.com/plan/guest-services/stroller-rental

Tickets and Packages
http://disneyland.disney.go.com/buy

Transportation
http://disneyland.disney.go.com/plan/guest-services/transportation

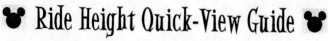

☙ Ride Height Quick-View Guide ☙

Most attractions at Disneyland Resort have no height restrictions. However, for the safety of guests, the rides below require riders to meet the following minimum height requirements.

32" (81cm) or Taller
Autopia, Luigi's Flying Tires, Mater's Junkyard Jamboree

35" (89cm) or Taller
Gadget's Go Coaster

36" (91cm) or Taller
Tuck and Roll's Drive 'Em Buggies

40" (102cm) or Taller
Big Thunder Mountain Railroad, Jumpin' Jellyfish, Radiator Springs Racers, Silly Symphony Swings Soarin' Over California, Space Mountain, Splash Mountain, The Twilight Zone Tower of Terror

42" (107cm) or Taller
Goofy's Sky School, Grizzly River Rapids, Matterhorn Bobsleds

46" (117cm) or Taller
Indiana Jones Adventure

48" (122cm) or Taller
California Screamin'

A dream is a wish your heart makes...

About the Author

When not visiting, writing about, talking about and dreaming about Disneyland, David Edgerton works as an advertising strategist and copywriter.

Working primarily in broadcast advertising (TV, Radio, online and social media), David has collected dozens of honors for creative excellence including ADDY, New York Festival and Emmy Awards.

David is also stepfather to two amazing young women. He lives with his partner and their Jack Russell terrier, Peanut, near Seattle, Washington.

Your questions, comments and suggestions are welcome. Write to: tearfree.disneyland@yahoo.com or join us on Facebook and Twitter.